interchange

FIFTH EDITION

1

Workbook

Jack C. Richards
with Jonathan Hull and Susan Proctor

CAMBRIDGE
UNIVERSITY PRESS

Shaftesbury Road, Cambridge CB2 8EA, United Kingdom

One Liberty Plaza, 20th Floor, New York, NY 10006, USA

477 Williamstown Road, Port Melbourne, VIC 3207, Australia

314–321, 3rd Floor, Plot 3, Splendor Forum, Jasola District Centre, New Delhi – 110025, India

103 Penang Road, #05-06/07, Visioncrest Commercial, Singapore 238467

Torre de los Parques, Colonia Tlacoquemécatl del Valle, Mexico City CP 03200, Mexico

Cambridge University Press & Assessment is a department of the University of Cambridge.

We share the University's mission to contribute to society through the pursuit of education, learning and research at the highest international levels of excellence.

www.cambridge.org
Information on this title: www.cambridge.org/9781316622476

First published 1990
Second edition 1997
Third edition 2005
Fourth edition 2013
Fifth edition 2017
Fifth edition update published 2021

40 39 38 37

Printed in Italy by L.E.G.O. S.p.A.

A catalogue record for this publication is available from the British Library.

ISBN   978-1-009-04044-0   Student's Book 1 with eBook
ISBN   978-1-009-04047-1   Student's Book 1A with eBook
ISBN   978-1-009-04048-8   Student's Book 1B with eBook
ISBN   978-1-009-04063-1   Student's Book 1 with Digital Pack
ISBN   978-1-009-04064-8   Student's Book 1A with Digital Pack
ISBN   978-1-009-04065-5   Student's Book 1B with Digital Pack
ISBN   978-1-316-62247-6   Workbook 1
ISBN   978-1-316-62254-4   Workbook 1A
ISBN   978-1-316-62266-7   Workbook 1B
ISBN   978-1-108-40606-2   Teacher's Edition 1
ISBN   978-1-316-62226-1   Class Audio 1
ISBN   978-1-009-04066-2   Full Contact 1 with Digital Pack
ISBN   978-1-009-04067-9   Full Contact 1A with Digital Pack
ISBN   978-1-009-04068-6   Full Contact 1B with Digital Pack
ISBN   978-1-108-40306-1   Presentation Plus 1

Additional resources for this publication at cambridgeone.org

Contents

Credits

Illustrations

Pablo Gallego (Beehive Illustration): 42, 53, 65, 78, 91; Thomas Girard (Good Illustration): 3, 25, 50, 72, 92; Quino Marin (The Organisation): 2, 47, 54, 66; Gavin Reece (New Division): 15, 48, 52(B); Paul Williams (Sylvie Poggio Artists): 51.

Photos

Back cover (woman with whiteboard): Jenny Acheson/Stockbyte/GettyImages; Back cover (whiteboard): Nemida/GettyImages; Back cover (man using phone): Betsie Van Der Meer/Taxi/GettyImages; Back cover (woman smiling): PeopleImages.com/DigitalVision/GettyImages; Back cover (name tag): Tetra Images/GettyImages; Back cover (handshake): David Lees/Taxi/GettyImages; p. 1: Jon Feingersh/Blend Images/Brand X Pictures/GettyImages; p. 4 (TL): Juanmonino/iStock/GettyImages Plus/GettyImages; p. 4 (BL): Caiaimage/Chris Ryan/OJO+/GettyImages; p. 4 (TR): XiXinXing/GettyImages; p. 4 (BR): powerofforever/E+/GettyImages; p. 5: PeopleImages/DigitalVision/GettyImages; p. 6: Martin Barraud/Caiaimage/GettyImages; p. 7 (photo 1): Jetta Productions/Blend Images/GettyImages; p. 7 (photo 2): Oleksandr Rupeta/NurPhoto/GettyImages; p. 7 (photo 3): Hill Street Studios/Blend Images/GettyImages; p. 7 (photo 4): Jupiterimages/Photolibrary/GettyImages; p. 8: Monty Rakusen/Cultura/GettyImages; p. 9: Matt Hage/Design Pics/First Light/GettyImages; p. 10 (TL): Digital Vision/DigitalVision/GettyImages; p. 10 (TR): Hybrid Images/Cultura/GettyImages; p. 10 (BR): kali9/E+/GettyImages; p. 11: kali9/E+/GettyImages; p. 12 (T): Hybrid Images/Cultura/GettyImages; p. 12 (BL): Visage/Stockbyte/GettyImages; p. 12 (BC): segawa7/iStock/GettyImages Plus/GettyImages; p. 12 (BR): asterix0597/E+/GettyImages; p. 13: Westend61/GettyImages; p. 14: Robert Niedring/Alloy/GettyImages; p. 16 (silver earrings): JohnGollop/iStock/GettyImages Plus/GettyImages; p. 16 (gold earrings): cobalt/iStock/GettyImages Plus/GettyImages; p. 16 (leather coat): bonetta/iStock/GettyImages Plus/GettyImages; p. 16 (wool coat): DonNichols/E+/GettyImages; p. 16 (orange shirt): rolleiflextlr/iStock/GettyImages Plus/GettyImages; p. 16 (gray shirt): popovaphoto/iStock/GettyImages Plus/GettyImages; p. 16 (cotton dresses): Evgenii Karamyshev/Hemera/GettyImages Plus/GettyImages; p. 16 (silk dresses): Paolo_Toffanin/iStock/GettyImages Plus/GettyImages; p. 17 (gold ring): Image Source/GettyImages; p. 17 (silver ring): ProArtWork/E+/GettyImages; p. 17 (tablet): luismmolina/E+/GettyImages; p. 17 (laptop computer): Howard Kingsnorth/The Image Bank/GettyImages; p. 17 (hiking boots): AlexRaths/iStock/GettyImages Plus/GettyImages; p. 17 (sneakers): badmanproduction/iStock/GettyImages Plus/GettyImages; p. 17 (wool gloves): popovaphoto/iStock/GettyImages Plus/GettyImages; p. 17 (leather gloves): Hugh Threlfall/Stockbyte/GettyImages; p. 17 (black sunglasses): Vladimir Liverts/Hemera/GettyImages Plus/GettyImages; p. 17 (white sunglasses): Dimedrol68/iStock/GettyImages Plus/GettyImages; p. 18 (photo 3): csfotoimages/iStock/GettyImages Plus/GettyImages; p. 18 (photo 1): Donald Iain Smith/Moment/GettyImages; p. 18 (photo 4): goir/iStock/GettyImages Plus/GettyImages; p. 18 (photo 2): Marc Romanelli/Blend Images/GettyImages; p. 19 (T): Larry Busacca/GettyImages Entertainment/GettyImages North America/GettyImages; p. 19 (B): Steve Granitz/WireImage/GettyImages; p. 20 (photo 1): Brian Bahr/GettyImages North America/GettyImages; p. 20 (photo 2): Phillip Faraone/GettyImages North America/GettyImages; p. 20 (photo 3): Anthony Harvey/GettyImages Entertainment/GettyImages Europe/GettyImages; p. 20 (photo 4): Taylor Hill/FilmMagic/GettyImages; p. 20 (BR): Jon Kopaloff/FilmMagic/GettyImages; p. 21 (R): DianaHirsch/E+/GettyImages; p. 21 (L): ILM/Universal Studios/GettyImages; p. 23 (T): Shirlaine Forrest/WireImage/GettyImages; p. 23 (B): Moof/Cultura/GettyImages; p. 24 (T): Mike Windle/GettyImages Entertainment/GettyImagesNorth America/GettyImages; p. 24 (B): Donald Miralle/DigitalVision/GettyImages; p. 26: Copyright Anek/Moment/GettyImages; p. 27 (photo 1): Echo/Cultura/GettyImages; p. 27 (photo 2): Juice Images/Cultura/GettyImages; p. 27 (photo 3): Christopher Hope-Fitch/Moment/GettyImages; p. 27 (photo 4): sjenner13/iStock/GettyImages Plus/GettyImages; p. 27 (photo 5): Hero Images/GettyImages; p. 30 (L): Soumen Nath Photography/Moment Open/GettyImages; p. 30 (R): Chaos/The Image Bank/GettyImages; p. 31 (L): Tetra Images/GettyImages; p. 31 (R): John Freeman/Dorling Kindersley/GettyImages; p. 33 (T): Westend61/GettyImages; p. 33 (B): Adam Gault/Photodisc/GettyImages; p. 34 (T): Camilla Watson/AWL Images/GettyImages; p. 34 (C): Stephen McCarthy/Sportsfile/GettyImages; p. 34 (B): PhotoAlto/Laurence Mouton/PhotoAlto Agency RF Collections/GettyImages; p. 35: Koji Aoki/Aflo/GettyImages; p. 36: PeopleImages/DigitalVision/GettyImages; p. 37: Jan Speiser/EyeEm/GettyImages; p. 38 (L): PeopleImages/DigitalVision/GettyImages; p. 38 (R): asiseeit/E+/GettyImages; p. 40 (T): PRASIT CHANSAREEKORN/Moment/GettyImages; p. 40 (B): Tuul and Bruno Morandi/Photolibrary/GettyImages; p. 41 (T): Boy_Anupong/Moment/GettyImages; p. 41 (B): John W Banagan/Lonely Planet Images/GettyImages; p. 46 (L): Allison Michael Orenstein/The Image Bank/GettyImages; p. 46 (R): Plume Creative/DigitalVision/GettyImages; p. 49: Jim Franco/Taxi/GettyImages; p. 52 (boots): StockPhotosArt/iStock/GettyImages Plus/GettyImages; p. 52 (cap): ljpat/E+/GettyImages; p. 52 (dress): pidjoe/E+/GettyImages; p. 52 (high heels): LOVE_LIFE/iStock/GettyImages Plus/GettyImages; p. 52 (jeans): gofotograf/iStock/GettyImages Plus/GettyImages; p. 52 (jewelry): DEA/L. DOUGLAS/De Agostini Editorial/GettyImages; p. 52 (necktie): Wilshirelmages/E+/GettyImages; p. 52 (shirt): Alex Cao/Photodisc/GettyImages; p. 52 (shorts): stocksnapper/iStock/GettyImages Plus/GettyImages; p. 52 (sneakers): Tevarak/iStock/GettyImages Plus/GettyImages;

p. 52 (suit): bonetta/iStock/GettyImages Plus/GettyImages; p. 52 (T-shirt): GaryAlvis/E+/GettyImages; p. 55 (T): Blake Little/Stone/GettyImages; p. 55 (C): Jenner Images/Moment Open/GettyImages; p. 55 (B): Kevin Kozicki/Image Source/GettyImages; p. 56: Barry Austin Photography/Iconica/GettyImages; p. 57 (photo 1): sutichak/iStock/GettyImages Plus/GettyImages; p. 57 (photo 2): Koichi Kamoshida/Photolibrary/GettyImages; p. 57 (photo 3): Westend61/GettyImages; p. 57 (photo 4): Paul Bradbury/OJO Images/GettyImages; p. 57 (photo 5): Jan Hetfleisch/GettyImages Europe/GettyImages; p. 57 (photo 6): Halfdark/GettyImages; p. 58 (T): Jupiterimages/Photos.com/GettyImages Plus/GettyImages; p. 58 (B): Nmaverick/iStock/GettyImages Plus/GettyImages; p. 59 (text messaging): skynesher/E+/GettyImages; p. 59 (rugby match): Stewart Cohen/Photolibrary/GettyImages; p. 59 (sushi): Steve Brown Photography/Photolibrary/GettyImages; p. 59 (houston): Gavin Hellier/Photographer's Choice/GettyImages; p. 60: Sam Edwards/Caiaimage/GettyImages; p. 61 (L): Martin Puddy/Stone/GettyImages; p. 61 (R): Karina Wang/Photographer's Choice/GettyImages; p. 62 (L): jimkruger/iStock/GettyImages Plus/GettyImages; p. 62 (C): AzmanL/iStock/GettyImages Plus/GettyImages; p. 62 (R): Jonas Gratzer/LightRocket/GettyImages; p. 63 (T): Alberto Manuel Urosa Toledano/Moment/GettyImages; p. 63 (B): DUCEPT Pascal/hemis.fr/GettyImages; p. 64 (BL): Sungjin Kim/Moment Open/GettyImages; p. 64 (TC): RODRIGO BUENDIA/AFP/GettyImages; p. 64 (BR): Andrea Pistolesi/Photolibrary/GettyImages; p. 65: JTB/UIG/GettyImages; p. 68: BSIP/UIG/GettyImages; p. 69: KidStock/Blend Images/GettyImages; p. 70: YinYang/E+/GettyImages; p. 71: Ariel Skelley/Blend Images/GettyImages; p. 73 (photo 1): Peter Dazeley/Photographer's Choice/GettyImages; p. 73 (photo 2): whitewish/E+/GettyImages; p. 73 (photo 3): Chuck Kahn/EyeEm/GettyImages; p. 73 (photo 4): lisafx/iStock/GettyImages Plus/GettyImages; p. 73 (photo 5): TUGIO MURATA/amanaimagesRF/GettyImages; p. 73 (photo 6): Creative Crop/DigitalVision/GettyImages; p. 74 (greasy): David Crunelle/EyeEm/GettyImages; p. 74 (bland): Howard Shooter/GettyImages; p. 74 (rich): Johner Images/GettyImages; p. 74 (salty): Creativ Studio Heinemann/GettyImages; p. 74 (healthy): Verdina Anna/Moment/GettyImages; p. 75 (Carlota): andresr/E+/GettyImages; p. 75 (Luka): NicolasMcComber/E+/GettyImages; p. 75 (Adam): David Harrigan/Canopy/GettyImages; p. 76 (broccoli): Kevin Summers/Photographer's Choice/GettyImages; p. 76 (sushi): Food Image Source/StockFood Creative/GettyImages; p. 76 (cream cone): dlerick/E+/GettyImages; p. 77: gchutka/E+/GettyImages; p. 79 (T): Richard Roscoe/Stocktrek Images/GettyImages; p. 79 (C): www.sierralara.com/Moment/GettyImages; p. 79 (B): Yevgen Timashov/Cultura/GettyImages; p. 80: Ulf Andersen/GettyImages Europe/GettyImages; p. 81 (Badwater Basin): David ToussaintMoment/GettyImages; p. 81 (Suez Canal): Jacques Marais/Gallo Images/GettyImages; p. 81 (Mount Waialeale): M Swiet Productions/Moment Open/GettyImages; p. 82: Christian Vorhofer/imageBROKER/GettyImages; p. 83 (Angel Falls): Jane Sweeney/AWL Images/GettyImages; p. 83 (Yangtze River): View Stock/GettyImages; p. 83 (Antarctica): Michael Nolan/robertharding/GettyImages; p. 83 (Rain forest): JohnnyLye/iStock/GettyImages Plus/GettyImages; p. 83 (Grand Canyon): Stephanie Hohmann/EyeEm/GettyImages; p. 84: GlobalP/iStock/GettyImages Plus/GettyImages; p. 86: Emilio Cobos/Euroleague Basketball/GettyImages; p. 87 (go to park): Feverpitched/iStock/GettyImages Plus/GettyImages; p. 87 (go to concerts): Yuri_Arcurs/DigitalVision/GettyImages; p. 87 (have parties): SolStock/E+/GettyImages; p. 87 (see plays): VisitBritain/Eric Nathan/Britain On View/GettyImages; p. 87 (watch horror movies): Crazytang/E+/GettyImages; p. 87 (go on picnics): Kentaroo Tryman/Maskot/GettyImages; p. 88 (Hannah): Dianne Avery Photography/GettyImages; p. 88 (Pablo): Jacqueline Veissid/Blend Images/GettyImages; p. 88 (Richard): Laura Doss/Image Source/GettyImages; p. 88 (Lien): iPandastudio/iStock/GettyImages Plus/GettyImages; p. 88 (Kalil): Juanmonino/E+/GettyImages; p. 88 (Rachel): Westend61/GettyImages; p. 88 (Eliana): billnoll/E+/GettyImages; p. 88 (Daichi): petekarici/iStock/GettyImages Plus/GettyImages; p. 90: ichaka/E+/GettyImages; p. 93 (L): Paul Bradbury/Caiaimage/GettyImages; p. 93 (TR): Hero Images/GettyImages; p. 93 (CR): Hero Images/DigitalVision/GettyImages; p. 94: Zero Creatives/Cultura/GettyImages; p. 95 (T): DragonImages/iStock/GettyImages Plus/GettyImages; p. 95 (C): agentry/iStock/GettyImages Plus/GettyImages; p. 95 (B): Digital Vision/Photodisc/GettyImages; p. 96: Deb Snelson/Moment/GettyImages.

1 Where are you from?

1 | Write about yourself.

My first name is _____.   Please call me _____.

My last name is _____.   I'm from _____.

2 | Put the words in order to make questions. Then answer the questions.

1. class   your   how   English   is

   A: _How is your English class_ ?

   B: _It's pretty interesting_ .

2. name   teacher's   your   what's

   A: _____ ?

   B: _____ .

3. from   your   teacher   where   is

   A: _____ ?

   B: _____ .

4. your   what   friends'   are   names

   A: _____ ?

   B: _____ .

5. classmates   what   your   are   like

   A: _____ ?

   B: _____ .

3 Choose the correct responses.

1. **A:** Hi, I'm Diane.

   B: _Oh, hi. I'm Peter._

   • Oh, hi. I'm Peter.

   • What do people call you?

2. **A:** My name is Bill Matory.

   B: _____

   • Nice to meet you, Bill.

   • Let's go and say hello.

3. **A:** Hello. I'm a new student here.

   B: _____

   • Thanks.

   • Welcome.

4. **A:** I'm sorry. What's your name again?

   B: _____

   • P-A-R-K.

   • Eun-ha Park.

5. **A:** How do you spell your first name?

   B: _____

   • I'm Akira.

   • A-K-I-R-A.

6. **A:** What do people call you?

   B: _____

   • It's Angela Young.

   • Everyone calls me Angie.

4 Look at the answers. What are the questions?

1. **Agent:** What _'s your name?_

   Silvia: My name's Silvia.

2. **Agent:** What _____

   Silvia: My last name's Garcia.

3. **Agent:** Who _____

   Silvia: That's my husband.

4. **Agent:** What _____

   Silvia: His name is Gustavo.

5. **Agent:** Where _____

   Silvia: We're from Venezuela.

6. **Agent:** Who _____

   Silvia: They're my children.

5 Choose the correct words.

1. That's Antonio. _____He_____ is in my class. (He / His)

2. I'm from Barcelona, Spain. _____ is a beautiful city. (It / It's)

3. Excuse me. What's _____ last name again? (you / your)

4. They're my classmates. _____ names are Jill and Tae-min. (They / Their)

5. _____ name is Naoko. Please call me Nao. (I / My)

6. This is Ellen's husband. _____ name is Tim. (His / Her)

7. My parents are on vacation. _____ are in Australia. (We / They)

8. We have English at 10:00. _____ classroom number is 108-C. (Our / We)

6 Complete this conversation with *am*, *are*, or *is*.

Amber: Who _____are_____ the men over there, Ethan?

Ethan: Oh, they _____ on my baseball team. Let me introduce you. Hi, Pablo, this _____ Amber Fox.

Pablo: Nice to meet you, Amber.

Amber: Nice to meet you, too. Where _____ you from?

Pablo: I _____ from Cuba.

Ethan: And this _____ Marco. He _____ from Brazil.

Lisa: Hi, Marco.

7 Hello and welcome!

A Read these four student biographies. Then complete the chart below.

>>> INTERNATIONAL LANGUAGE SCHOOL <<<

Every month, we meet new students at the school. This month, we want to introduce four new students to you. Please say "hello" to them!

Rafael is in English 101. He is from Puebla, Mexico. His first language is Spanish, and he also speaks a little French. He wants to be on the school volleyball team. He says he doesn't play very well, but he wants to learn!

Su-yin is in English 102. She is from Wuhan, China. She says she writes and reads English pretty well, but she needs a lot of practice speaking English. Her first language is Chinese. She wants to play volleyball on the school team.

Fatima is in English 103. She is from Tunis, Tunisia. She speaks Arabic and French. She is an engineering student. She wants to be an engineer. She says she doesn't play any sports. She wants to make a lot of new friends in her class.

Finally, meet **Arun**. He is in Fatima's class. He says he speaks English well, but his writing isn't very good! Arun is from Chennai, India, and his first language is Hindi. He is a soccer player, and he wants to be on the school soccer team.

Name	Where from	Languages	Sports
1. Rafael			
2.	Tunis, Tunisia		
3.		English and Chinese	
4.			soccer

B Write a short biography of a classmate.

_____

_____

_____

_____

_____

8 Choose the correct sentences to complete this conversation.

- ☐ You, too. Talk to you later.
- ☑ Hi, Stacey. I'm Omar. How are you?
- ☐ I really like biology.
- ☐ Yes, I am. I'm an exchange student from Egypt.
- ☐ Yes, he is. We're in Biology 300. Is he your friend?

Stacey: Hello, I'm Stacey.

Omar: _Hi, Stacey. I'm Omar. How are you?_

Stacey: Pretty good, thanks. Are you a student here?

Omar: _____

Stacey: Welcome. Do you like it here? What's your favorite subject?

Omar: _____

Stacey: Oh, really? Is Ben Jones in your class?

Omar: _____

Stacey: No, he's my brother! Actually, I have to go meet him now. Nice to meet you, Omar.

Omar: _____

9 Complete this conversation. Use contractions where possible.

Grammar note: Contractions

Do not use contractions for short answers with **Yes.**

Are you from Argentina?	Is he from Greece?
Yes, I am. (*not* Yes, I'm.)	Yes, he is. (*not* Yes, he's.)

Alex: Hello. ___I'm___ Alex Robles.
And this is my sister Celia.

Paola: Hi. _____ Paola Vieira.

Celia: Are you from South America, Paola?

Paola: Yes, _____. _____ from Brazil.
Where are you both from?

Alex: _____ from Puerto Rico.

Paola: Are you from San Juan?

Celia: No, _____. _____ from
Ponce. By the way, are you in English
101?

Paola: No, _____. I'm in English 102.

10 Look at the answers. What are the questions?

1. A: _Who's Allison?_

   B: Allison is my best friend.

2. A: _____

   B: My favorite school subject is history.

3. A: _____

   B: No, we're not from Germany. We're from Switzerland.

4. A: _____

   B: Yes, it's an interesting class.

5. A: _____

   B: Yes, Mary and Yuka are in my class.

6. A: _____

   B: Ryan is funny and friendly.

7. A: _____

   B: No, Ms. Rogers isn't my English teacher. She's my math teacher.

11 Read the expressions. Which ones say "hello" and which ones say "good-bye"?

	Hello	Good-bye
1. How are you?	☑	☐
2. See you tomorrow.	☐	☐
3. Good night.	☐	☐
4. Good morning.	☐	☐
5. Talk to you later.	☐	☐
6. How's it going?	☐	☐
7. Have a good day.	☐	☐
8. What's up?	☐	☐

12 Answer these questions about yourself. Use contractions where possible.

1. Are you on vacation?   _____

2. Is your teacher from Canada?   _____

3. Is your first name popular?   _____

4. Is your English class in the morning? _____

5. Are you from Asia?   _____

6. Are you a student at a university?   _____

2 What do you do?

1 Match the correct words to make sentences.

1. A cashier   _d_   a. helps sick people.
2. A vendor   _____   b. takes care of animals.
3. A babysitter _____   c. sells things.
4. A doctor   _____   d. takes money and gives change.
5. A tutor   _____   e. takes care of children.
6. A pet sitter _____   f. helps students with their school work.

2 Write sentences using *He* or *She*.

1. I'm a mechanic. I fix cars. I work in a garage.
   He's a mechanic. He fixes cars.
   He works in a garage.

2. I'm a cook. I cook food. I work in a restaurant.
   _She _____
   _____

3. I'm a math teacher. I teach math to students.
   I work in a school.
   _She _____
   _____

4. I'm a taxi driver. I drive a car. I take people to
   places they want to go.
   _He _____
   _____

3 Write *a* or *an* in the correct places.

> **Grammar note: Articles *a* and *an***
>
> **Use *a* + singular noun before a consonant sound.**
>
> **Use *an* + singular noun before a vowel sound.**
>
> He is **a c**arpenter. He is **an a**ccountant.
>
> He is **a g**ood carpenter. He is **an e**xpensive accountant.
>
> **Do not use *a* or *an* + plural nouns.**
>
> They are good carpenter**s**. They are expensive accountant**s**.

1. He's ^a carpenter. He works for ^a construction company. He builds schools and houses.
2. She's office manager. She works for large company. It's interesting job.
3. He works in restaurant. He's server. He's also part-time student. He takes business class in the evening.
4. She works for travel company. She arranges tours. She's travel agent.
5. He has difficult job. He's flight attendant. He works on airplane.

4 Choose someone in your family. Write about his or her job.

_____

_____

_____

_____

5 Complete this conversation with the correct words.

Tiffany: What ____*does*____ your brother _____, exactly?
(do / does)   (do / does)

Kate: He _____ for the city. He's a firefighter.
(work / works)

Tiffany: How _____ he _____ it?
(do / does)   (like / likes)

Kate: It's an interesting job. He _____ it very much.
(like / likes)

But he _____ long hours. And what _____ you _____?
(work / works)   (do / does)   (do / does)

Tiffany: I'm a student. I _____ geography.
(study / studies)

Kate: Oh, really? Where _____ you _____ to school?
(do / does)   (go / goes)

Tiffany: I _____ to Matthews University. My brother _____ there, too.
(go / goes)   (go / goes)

Kate: Really? And what _____ he _____?
(do / does)   (study / studies)

Tiffany: He _____ graphic design.
(study / studies)

Kate: That sounds interesting.

6 Complete the questions in this conversation.

Tom: _Where do you work?_

Ray: I work for Brady Corporation.

Tom: And what _____
there?

Ray: I'm an accountant.

Tom: An accountant? How
_____

Ray: I like numbers, so it's a great job.
And what _____

Tom: I'm a teacher.

Ray: Really? What _____

Tom: I teach accounting!

7 Interesting jobs

Read these two interviews. Answer the questions.

Today, **Job Talk** interviews two people with interesting jobs.

Job Talk: Oliver, where do you work?

Oliver: Well, I guess I work in the sky.

Job Talk: In the sky? What do you do?

Oliver: I'm a flight attendant. I work on the international flight from Miami to Recife, Brazil.

Job Talk: That's really interesting. What do you like best about your job?

Oliver: I really like to travel and to meet people. So my job is perfect for me.

Job Talk: Do you speak Portuguese?

Oliver: I speak a little. I carry my dictionary everywhere I go!

Job Talk: What do you do, Lucy?

Lucy: I'm a security guard at Matthews University.

Job Talk: That sounds difficult. What is the hardest thing about your job?

Lucy: Well, people break the rules at the university, and I have to stop them.

Job Talk: Are people unfriendly to you?

Lucy: Sometimes, but most of the students are very nice.

Job Talk: And what do you like best about your job?

Lucy: Well, some days the university is quiet. I get to read a lot of books!

1. What does Oliver do?   He _____
2. Where does he work? _____
3. How does Oliver learn Portuguese? _____
4. What does Lucy do?   She _____
5. Where does she work? _____
6. What is the hardest part of her job? _____

8 Meet Patricio. Write questions about him using *What*, *Where*, *When*, and *How*.

1. _What does he do?_ _____
2. _____
3. _____
4. _____

Mercy Hospital

Patricio Cardozo
Registered Nurse,
Night Shift

9 How does Patricio spend his weekends? Complete this paragraph with the words from the box.

☐ around	☐ at	☐ before	☐ early
☐ in	☐ late	☑ on	☐ until

Everyone knows Patricio at the hospital. Patricio is a part-time nurse. He works at night on weekends. _____On_____ Saturdays and Sundays, Patricio sleeps most of the day and wakes up a little _____ nine _____ the evening, usually at 8:45 or 8:50. He has breakfast very late, _____ 9:30 or 10:00 P.M.! He watches television _____ eleven o'clock and then starts work _____ midnight. _____ in the morning, usually around 5:00 A.M., he leaves work, has a little snack, goes home, goes to bed, and sleeps _____. It's a perfect schedule for Patricio. He's a pre-med student on weekdays at a local college.

10 Choose the correct words to complete the sentences.

1. Avery is a tour guide. She _____takes_____ (answers / takes / writes) people on tours.

2. Stella _____ (does / goes / starts) to bed after midnight.

3. Bonnie _____ (answers / gets / starts) up early in the morning.

4. What _____ (does / goes / serves) your sister do?

5. Roland _____ (answers / serves / starts) work at 8:00 A.M.

6. My brother works in a bookstore. He _____ (answers / sells / works) books and magazines.

7. The Havana Garden restaurant _____ (serves / takes / writes) good Cuban food.

8. Dan _____ (serves / does / works) his school work on his new computer.

9. Nunu _____ (goes / sells / writes) about 30 emails a day.

10. David is a receptionist. He _____ (answers / starts / types) the phone and greets people.

11. Miguel _____ (does / takes / works) in a restaurant.

11 Choose the sentences in the box that have the same meaning as the sentences below.

- ☐ He goes to the university.
- ☐ She cares for people's pets.
- ☐ She stays up late.
- ☐ What does he do?
- ☑ She's a fitness instructor.
- ☐ He works part-time.

1. She teaches exercise classes.

   She's a fitness instructor.

2. What's his job?

   _____

3. She's a pet sitter.

   _____

4. He's a student.

   _____

5. She goes to bed at midnight.

   _____

6. He works three hours every day.

   _____

12 Fill in the missing words or phrases from these job advertisements.

1. ☐ at night
   ☐ part-time
   ☑ servers
   ☐ weekends

2. ☐ interesting
   ☐ Japanese
   ☐ tours
   ☐ student

3. ☐ at
   ☐ in
   ☐ manager
   ☐ weekends

Help Wanted

Larry's Diner needs _____servers_____. Work during the day or _____, weekdays or _____, full-time or _____. Call 901–555–1977.

_____ job for a language _____. Take people on _____. Evenings only. Need good English and _____ skills. Email Brenda at Brenda44@cup.org.

We need a great office _____! Work Monday through Friday, no _____. Start work _____ 9:00 _____ the morning.

3 How much are these?

1 Choose the correct sentences to complete this conversation.

☐ Oh, James. Thank you very much.　　☐ Well, I like it, but it's expensive.

☐ Which one?　　✓ Which ones?　　☐ Yes. But I don't really like yellow.

James: Look at those pants, Linda.

Linda: _Which ones?_

James: The yellow ones over there. They're nice.

Linda: _____

James: Hmm. Well, what about that sweater? It's perfect for you.

Linda: _____

James: This blue one.

Linda: _____

James: Hey, let me buy it for you. It's a present!

Linda: _____

2 Complete these conversations with *How much is/are . . . ?* and *this, that, these,* or *those.*

1. **A:** _How much is this_ blouse right here?

   B: It's $47.95.

2. **A:** _____ glasses over there?

   B: They're $87.

3. **A:** _____ sneakers right here?

   B: They're $79.99.

4. **A:** _____ cat over there?

   B: That's *my* cat, and he's not for sale!

3 Write the plurals of these words.

1. ring ____rings____

2. glove _____

3. party _____

4. boy _____

5. tie _____

6. box _____

7. scarf _____

8. blouse _____

9. T-shirt _____

10. hairbrush _____

11. computer _____

12. dress _____

4 What do you think of these prices? Write a response.

That's cheap.   That's not bad.   That's reasonable.   That's pretty expensive!

1. $250 for a wool sweater

That's pretty expensive! _____

2. $30 for a silk tie

_____

3. $180 for a cotton dress

_____

4. $40 for a gold necklace

_____

5. $15 for three T-shirts

_____

6. $80 for a leather belt

_____

5 Choose the correct words to complete the conversations.

1. Shirley: I like _____*those*_____ earrings over there.
(that / those)

   Clerk: Which _____?
(one / ones)

Shirley: The small gold _____.
(one / ones)

   Clerk: _____ $399.
(It's / They're)

Shirley: Oh, they're expensive!

2. George: Excuse me. How much
are _____ pants?
(that / those)

   Clerk: _____ only $65.
(It's / They're)

George: And how much is _____ shirt?
(this / these)

   Clerk: Which _____?
(one / ones)

They're all different.

George: This green _____.
(one / ones)

   Clerk: _____ $47.
(It's / They're)

3.   **Clerk:** Good afternoon.

Martina: Oh, hi. How much is
_____ watch?
(this / these)

   Clerk: _____ $195.
(It's / They're)

Martina: And how much is
that _____?
(one / ones)

   Clerk: _____ $99.
(It's / They're)

Martina: That's not bad. I'll take it!

6 **What do you make from these materials? Complete the chart using words from the box. (You will use words more than once.)**

belt	boots	bracelet	button	gloves	hairbrush
jacket	necklace	pants	ring	shirt	

Cotton	Gold	Leather	Plastic	Silk	Wool
gloves					

7 **Make comparisons using the words given. Add *than* if necessary.**

1. A: Hey, look at these silver earrings! They're nice. And they're _____*cheaper than*_____ those gold earrings. (cheap)

B: But they're _____ the gold ones. (small)

A: Well, yeah. The gold ones are _____ the silver ones. (big) But $400 is a lot of money!

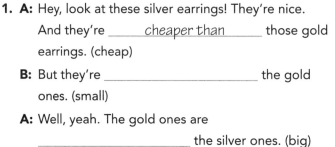
silver earrings

gold earrings

2. A: This leather coat is _____ the wool one. (attractive)

B: Yes, but the wool one is _____. (warm)

leather coat

wool coat

3. A: This orange shirt is an interesting color!

B: Yes, but the color is _____ the design. (pretty)

A: The design isn't bad.

B: I think the pattern on that gray shirt is _____ the pattern on this orange one. (good)

orange shirt

gray shirt

4. A: These cotton dresses are nice.

B: Yes, but the silk ones are _____. (nice)

A: They're also _____. (expensive)

cotton dresses

silk dresses

8 Complete the chart. Use the words from the box.

- ☑ boots
- ☐ bracelet
- ☐ dress
- ☐ earrings
- ☐ MP3 player
- ☐ necklace
- ☐ pants
- ☐ ring
- ☐ tablet
- ☐ television
- ☐ T-shirt
- ☐ smartphone

Clothing	Electronics	Jewelry
boots		

9 Answer these questions. Give your own information.

1	2	3	4	5
gold ring	tablet	hiking boots	wool gloves	black sunglasses
silver ring	laptop computer	sneakers	leather gloves	white sunglasses

1. Which ring do you prefer, the silver one or the gold one?

 I prefer the gold one.

2. Which one do you like more, the tablet or the laptop computer?

_____

3. Which ones do you like more, the hiking boots or the sneakers?

_____

4. Which ones do you prefer, the wool gloves or the leather gloves?

_____

5. Which sunglasses do you like better, the black ones or the white ones?

_____

10 Great gadgets!

A Read these ads. Match the pictures and descriptions.

1. _____   2. _____   3. _____   4. _____

a. Do you want to help the environment and do yard work at the same time?
    This machine knows when your lawn needs water. It waters your grass, and
    you don't have to do anything! Save time, save water, and save money!
    Only $124.99.

b. You can take this with you to the beach or on a picnic. No more uncomfortable
    towels or blankets! It fills with air in five minutes. Feel like you are sitting in
    your own living room in the great outdoors! Only $49.50.

c. What's a party without music? Indoors or outdoors, you can have a good
    time with this small item on a shelf or in a tree. Turn it down to set the mood,
    or turn it up to start the dancing! Only $299.99.

d. What's it like to swim like a fish? Now is your chance to find out! Put both feet
    in, get in the water, and feel what it's like to flap instead of kick. If you love to
    be in the water and dive deep, you need this! $36.

B Check (✓) True or False.

	True	False
1. The garden sensor waters your lawn when it needs more water.	☐	☐
2. The inflatable chair takes about five minutes to fill with air.	☐	☐
3. The Soundbook only works indoors.	☐	☐
4. You need two monofins, one for each foot.	☐	☐

C What's special about a gadget you have? Write a paragraph about it.

_____

_____

_____

_____

_____

_____

_____

4 Do you play the guitar?

1 **Check (✓) the boxes to complete the survey about music and TV.**

A Do you like these types of music?

	I love it!	It's OK.	I don't like it.
pop	☐	☐	☐
classical	☐	☐	☐
hip-hop	☐	☐	☐
rock	☐	☐	☐
jazz	☐	☐	☐

B Do you like these types of TV shows?

	I love them!	They're OK.	I don't like them.
talk shows	☐	☐	☐
reality shows	☐	☐	☐
sitcoms	☐	☐	☐
soap operas	☐	☐	☐
game shows	☐	☐	☐

2 **What's your opinion? Answer the questions with the expressions and pronouns in the box.**

Yes, I do. I love . . . I like . . . a lot. **No, I don't.** I don't like . . . very much. I can't stand . . .	**Object pronouns** him her it them

Kendrick Lamar

1. Do you like horror movies?
   Yes, I do. I like them a lot.

2. Do you like Kendrick Lamar?
   _____

3. Do you like heavy metal music?
   _____

4. Do you like mystery books?
   _____

5. Do you like video games?
   _____

6. Do you like Adele?
   _____

Adele

3 Choose the correct job for each picture.

☐ an actor   ☐ an athlete   ☐ a pop group   ☐ a singer

1. Hope Solo is _____

2. Fall Out Boy are _____

3. Chris Hemsworth is

_____

_____

4. Luke Bryan is

_____

_____

4 Complete these conversations.

1. **Ken:** _____Do_____ you _____like_____ pop music, Janet?

  Janet: Yes, I _____ it a lot. I'm a big fan of Beyoncé.

  Ken: Oh, _____ she play the guitar?

  Janet: No, she _____, but she's a great dancer.

2. **Alice:** _____ kind of music _____ your

  parents _____, Jack?

  Jack: They _____ country music.

  Alice: Who _____ they _____?
  Jason Aldean?

  Jack: No, they _____ like him very much. They prefer Carrie Underwood.

3. **Harold:** Kelly, who's your favorite female singer? _____ you _____
  Selena Gomez?

  Kelly: No, I _____. I can't stand her. I like Etana.

  Harold: I don't know her. What kind of music _____ she sing?

  Kelly: She _____ reggae. She's really great!

5 Complete these questions and write answers.

1. <u>What kinds</u> of movies do you like?   I like _____
2. _____ is your favorite movie?   My favorite _____
3. _____ of movies do you dislike? _____
4. _____ of TV shows do you like? _____
5. _____ is your favorite actor or actress? _____
6. _____ is your favorite song? _____
7. _____ is your favorite rock band? _____
8. _____ is your favorite video game? _____

6 What do you think? Answer the questions.

1. Which are more interesting, action movies or historical dramas?

_____

2. Which movies are more exciting, westerns or crime thrillers?

_____

3. Which do you like more, musicals or animated movies?

_____

4. Which do you prefer, romantic comedies or science fiction movies?

_____

5. Which are scarier, horror movies or thrillers?

_____

7 Verbs and nouns

A Which nouns often go with these verbs? Complete the chart. Use each noun only once.

listen to	play	watch
music		

- ☐ a basketball game
- ☐ the piano
- ☐ the guitar
- ☐ videos
- ☐ the radio
- ☐ R&B
- ☐ the drums
- ☑ music
- ☐ a movie

B Write a sentence using each verb in part A.

1. _____
2. _____
3. _____

8 Movie reviews

A Read the movie reviews. Write the type of movie for each review below the title.

comedy	historical drama	science fiction	crime thriller	horror
travel	documentary	romantic comedy	western	

Movie Reviews

Home   News   Reviews   Listings   Box Office   Sign in   Register

1 Ahead of Time

What are high school kids like in the future? This movie gives an answer. It's about a group of school kids in the year 2017. After class one day, they find a time machine behind the school. One of the teens sees a button marked "Year 2500" and presses it. They suddenly travel to the twenty-sixth century! They have many exciting adventures. But do they get back in time for school the next day? Watch and find out.

SCORE ★★★★☆

2 House of Laughs

This movie is about a group of six young people in London. They live in the same house in a suburb far from the city center. All of them come from different countries. They speak different languages and have different customs. What happens when they're all under one roof? Watch and laugh! The story is very funny, and the acting is very good. This movie is like a really good TV soap opera, but funnier.

SCORE ★★★★★

3 Coming Up for Air

The action never stops in this movie. Police officer Karen Montana wants to catch Mr. X, a notorious gold thief. Mr. X is stealing gold from an old shipwreck at the bottom of the ocean. The only way to catch him is under the water. But Montana's one weakness is that she can't swim and hates the water. Will she catch him? The plot isn't very good, but the surprise ending is worth waiting for. Watch for yourself.

SCORE ★★☆☆☆

B Write down the words in the review that helped you to decide what kind of movie it is.

1. Ahead of Time: _future,_____
2. House of Laughs: _____
3. Coming Up for Air: _____

9 Choose the correct responses.

1. A: What do you think of "The Voice"?

   B: <u>I'm not a real fan of the show.</u>

     • How about you?

     • I'm not a real fan of the show.

2. A: Do you like jazz music?

   B: _____

     • I can't stand it.

     • I can't stand them.

3. A: There's a soccer game tonight.

   B: _____

     • Thanks. I'd love to.

     • Great. Let's go.

4. A: Would you like to see a movie this weekend?

   B: _____

     • That sounds great!

     • I don't agree.

10 Yes or no?

A Fabiana is inviting friends to a movie. Do they accept the invitation or not?
Check (✓) *Yes* or *No* for each response.

Accept?	Yes	No
1. I'd love to. What time does it start?	✓	☐
2. Thanks, but I don't really like animated movies.	☐	☐
3. That sounds great. Where is it?	☐	☐
4. I'd love to, but I have to work until midnight.	☐	☐
5. Thanks. I'd really like to. When do you want to meet?	☐	☐

B Respond to the invitations.

1. I have tickets to a classical concert on Saturday. Would you like to go?

_____

2. There's a soccer game tonight. Do you want to go with me?

_____

3. Meghan Trainor is performing tomorrow at the stadium. Would you like to see her?

_____

11 Choose the correct phrases to complete these conversations.

1. **Eva:** _Do you like_ pop music, Anita?
   (Do you like / Would you like)

   Anita: Yes, I do. _____ it a lot.
   (I like / I'd like)

   Eva: There's an Ariana Grande concert on Friday.
   _____ to go with me?
   (Do you like / Would you like)

   Anita: Yes, _____! Thanks.
   (I love to / I'd love to)

2. **Marco:** There's a baseball game on TV tonight.

   _____ to come over and watch it?
   (Do you like / Would you like)

   Tony: _____, but I have to study tonight.
   (I like to / I'd like to)

   Marco: Well, _____ basketball?
   (do you like / would you like)

   Tony: Yes, _____. I love it!
   (I do / I would)

   Marco: There's a game on TV tomorrow at 3:00.

   _____ to watch that with me?
   (Do you like / Would you like)

   Tony: _____. Thanks!
   (I like to / I'd love to)

12 Rewrite these sentences. Find another way to say each sentence using the words given.

1. Do you like rap?

   What do you think of rap? (think of)

2. Chad doesn't like country music.

   _____ (can't stand)

3. I think soap operas are great!

   _____ (love)

4. Celia doesn't like new age music.

   _____ (be a fan of)

5. Do you want to go to a soccer match?

   _____ (would like)

5 What an interesting family!

1 **Which words are for males? Which are for females? Complete the chart.**

☑ aunt   ☐ husband   ☐ sister

☑ brother   ☐ mother   ☐ son

☐ daughter   ☐ nephew   ☐ uncle

☐ father   ☐ niece   ☐ wife

Males			Females		
brother			aunt		

2 **Complete this conversation. Use the present continuous of the verbs given.**

Jan: You look tired, Monica.

_____Are you studying_____ (study) late at night these days?

Monica: No, I'm not. My brother and sister _____ (stay) with me right now. They keep me up late every night.

Jan: Really, both of them? What _____ (do) this summer? _____ (take) classes, too?

Monica: No, they aren't. My brother is on vacation now, but he _____ (look) for a part-time job here.

Jan: What about your sister? _____ (work)?

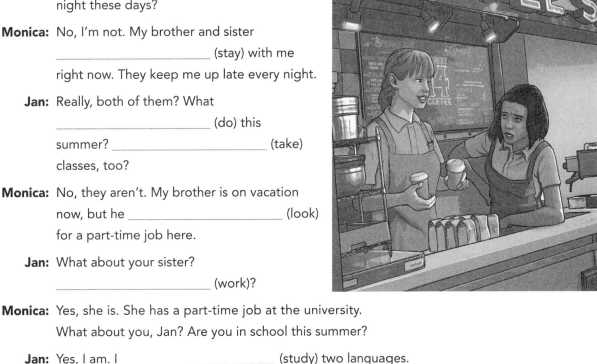

Monica: Yes, she is. She has a part-time job at the university. What about you, Jan? Are you in school this summer?

Jan: Yes, I am. I _____ (study) two languages.

Monica: Oh, _____ (take) Korean and Spanish again?

Jan: Well, I'm taking Korean, but now I _____ (start) Portuguese classes.

Monica: Really? That's exciting!

3 What is another way to say each sentence? Rewrite the sentences using the words in the box.

aunt	mother-in-law	~~uncle~~
granddaughter	son and daughter	wife

1. Anita is Marco's niece.

   Marco is Anita's uncle.

2. John is married to Ann.

   _____

3. My father's sister is a teacher.

   _____

4. We have two children.

   _____

5. My husband's mother is from Mexico.

   _____

6. Willie and Mabel are Brooke's grandparents.

   _____

4 Choose the correct sentences to complete the conversation.

- [ ] Yes, he is. He loves it there.
- [✓] No, I'm not. I'm living in Singapore now.
- [ ] Yes, we are. We really love Miami.
- [ ] Yes, I do. I like it a lot.
- [ ] No, they aren't. They're living in Atlanta now.

Singapore

Kathy: Are you still living in Miami, Martin?

Martin: _No, I'm not. I'm living in Singapore now._

Kathy: Wow! Do you like it?

Martin: _____

Kathy: And is your brother still working in Seoul?

Martin: _____

Kathy: And how about your parents? Are they still living in Florida?

Martin: _____ How about you and your family, Kathy? Are you still living here?

Kathy: _____

5 Complete these sentences. Use the simple present or the present continuous of the verbs given.

1. This is my cousin, Martin.

He _____*lives*_____ (live) in Houston, but

he _____ (visit) Peru this summer.

He _____ (take) cooking classes there.

2. And these are my parents.

They _____ (work) in Paris this year.

They _____ (be) on vacation right now.

3. Here's a photo of my grandparents.

They _____ (not work) now.

They _____ (be) retired.

4. This is my sister-in-law, Amanda.

She _____ (want) to start her own company.

She _____ (study) business in Australia right now.

5. And this is my nephew, George.

He _____ (go) to high school.

He _____ (like) history, but

he _____ (not like) chemistry.

6 Choose a friend or a family member. Write about him or her using the simple present and present continuous.

_____

_____

_____

_____

7 Home or away?

A Answer these questions. Then read the passage.

1. Read the title below. What do you think a "boomerang kid" is?

_____

2. Are you going to live at home when you leave school? Why or why not?

_____

BOOMERANG KIDS _____

Today in the United States, many young adults are returning home to live after they graduate from college. They are being called "boomerang kids," like the Australian hunting stick that comes back after you throw it. Many college graduates can't find the jobs they want right away. Some also have college loans to pay back. They don't have enough money to rent expensive apartments, so they go back home to live with their parents. While they live at home, they are working at jobs with low pay and trying to save money for the future.

Meanwhile, the parents of boomerang kids are feeling the challenges of having their adult children back home. Most understand the problems their kids are having with money and accept that they're living with them again. But their relationships are different now. Some parents expect their kids to keep following their rules and to help around the house. Young adults, on the other hand, want to be independent and to make their own decisions. This creates tension between parents and kids. These boomerangs go out as kids, but they come back as adults.

B Check (✓) True or False. For statements that are false, write the correct information.

Young Adults	True	False
1. "Boomerang kids" are college graduates who don't want to live at home. _____	☐	☐
2. Many college graduates are having a difficult time finding a good job. _____	☐	☐
3. College graduates who live at home can't save money for the future. _____	☐	☐

Parents	True	False
4. Parents are seeing that it can be difficult to have their "boomerang kids" live at home again. _____	☐	☐
5. Parents want to do everything for their kids like they did when they were younger. _____	☐	☐
6. Parents and kids mostly agree about the rules and expectations of the house. _____	☐	☐

8 Arrange the quantifiers from the most to the least.

- ☑ all
- ☐ few
- ☐ many
- ☐ most
- ☐ nearly all
- ☑ no
- ☐ some

1. _____ all _____
2. _____
3. _____
4. _____
5. _____
6. _____
7. _____ no _____

9 Rewrite these sentences about the United States using the quantifiers given.

1. Ninety percent of children go to public schools. Ten percent of children go to private schools.

   Most _children go to public schools._
   Few _____
   _____

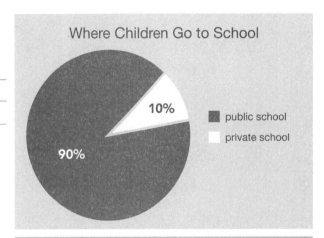

Where Children Go to School

10%
90%

- ■ public school
- □ private school

2. Sixty-two percent of young people go to college after they finish high school. Thirty-four percent of young people look for work.

   Many _____
   _____
   Some _____
   _____

What People Do After They Finish High School

4%
34%
62%

- ■ go to college
- □ look for work
- ■ other

3. Ninety-five percent of people over 65 like to talk to family and friends. Forty-three percent of people over 65 like to spend time on a hobby. Three percent of people over 65 like to play soccer.

   Not many _____
   _____
   A lot of _____
   _____
   Nearly all _____
   _____

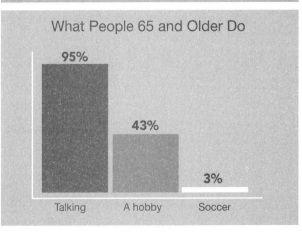

What People 65 and Older Do

95%
43%
3%

Talking   A hobby   Soccer

10 Choose the correct words or phrases to complete this paragraph.

In my country, some _____couples_____ (couples / cousins / relatives) get married fairly
young. Not many marriages _____ (break up / get divorced / stay together),
and nearly all _____ (divorced / married / single) people remarry. Elderly
couples often _____ (divorce again / move away / live at home) and take
care of their grandchildren.

11 Complete these sentences about your country. Use the words in the box.

all	a lot of	few	most	nearly all	no	some

1. _____ young people go to college.
2. _____ people study English.
3. _____ married couples have more than five children.
4. _____ elderly people have part-time jobs.
5. _____ students have full-time jobs.
6. _____ children go to school on Saturdays.

6 How often do you run?

1 **Complete the chart. Use words from the box.**

baseball	soccer	basketball	volleyball	football
walking	jogging	weight training	Pilates	yoga

Sports	Fitness activities
baseball	

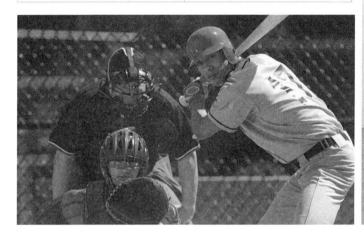

2 **Arrange these words to make sentences or questions.**

1. often   mornings   play   on   we   tennis   Saturday

   We often play tennis on Saturday mornings.

2. ever   Ryan   do   does   yoga

   _____?

3. go   do   often   swimming   how   you

   _____?

4. go   never   I   almost   jogging

   _____.

5. hardly   they   basketball   play   ever

   _____.

6. do   on   you   what   usually   Sundays   do

   _____?

3 Use these questions to complete the conversations: *How often do you . . . ?*
Do you ever . . . ? What do you usually . . . ?

1. **A:** _Do you ever go bowling?_

    B: Yes, I often go bowling on weekends.

2. **A:** _____

    B: Well, I usually do martial arts or watch TV after work.

3. **A:** _____

    B: Yes, I sometimes play sports on weekends – usually soccer.

4. **A:** _____

    B: I don't exercise very often at all.

5. **A:** _____

    B: No, I never go to the gym on Saturdays.

6. **A:** _____

    B: I usually go jogging four times a week.

4 Keeping fit?

A Check (✓) how often you do each of the things in the chart.

	Every day	Once or twice a week	Sometimes	Not very often	Never
do martial arts	☐	☐	☐	☐	☐
play basketball	☐	☐	☐	☐	☐
exercise	☐	☐	☐	☐	☐
go jogging	☐	☐	☐	☐	☐
go bowling	☐	☐	☐	☐	☐
play soccer	☐	☐	☐	☐	☐
go swimming	☐	☐	☐	☐	☐
do weight training	☐	☐	☐	☐	☐

B Write about your fitness habits using the information in the chart.

_____

_____

_____

_____

_____

_____

_____

5 Complete this conversation with the correct prepositions. Write them in the correct places.

Kelly: What time do you go swimming ^in the morning? (around / in / on)

Neil: I always go swimming 7:00. (at / for / on)

How about you, Kelly?

Kelly: I usually go swimming noon. (around / in / with)

I swim about 30 minutes. (at / for / until)

Neil: And do you also play sports your free time? (at / in / until)

Kelly: No, I usually go out my classmates. (around / for / with)

What about you?

Neil: I go to the gym Mondays and Wednesdays. (at / on / until)

And sometimes I go jogging weekends. (for / in / on)

Kelly: Wow! You really like to stay in shape.

6 Complete the sentences. Use the words from the box.

do	ice hockey	soccer	treadmill	goes	jogging
swimming	watches	~~exercises~~	shape	training	

1. Katie never ___exercises___ .
   She's a real couch potato.

2. How often do you _____ martial arts?

3. I like to stay in _____. I play sports every day.

4. Jeff does weight _____ every evening. He lifts 50-pound weights.

5. Arturo goes _____ twice a week. He usually runs about three miles.

6. Miho often _____ TV in the evening.

7. Maria is on the _____ team at her high school. She's good at passing the ball.

8. Judy never goes _____ when the water is cold.

9. Kyle often _____ bike riding on weekends.

10. I run on the _____ at the gym three times a week.

11. In Canada, many people like to play _____ outside in the winter.

A Read the descriptions of three unique sports that are played in different parts of the world. Which sport do you want to try? Why?

Capoeira

Capoeira is a sport that comes from Brazil. It is part martial art, part dance, and part game. The legs do most of the work in this sport. Capoeiristas kick, jump, and dance to the music of stringed instruments, drums, bells, and rattles. Although the two people are fighting and defending themselves, capoeira is really more about movement, speed, and knowing what your opponent is thinking.

Hurling

The game of hurling comes from Ireland. It is the fastest field sport in the world. Hurlers play on a field like soccer but use a stick and a small ball. The stick is used to carry or hit the ball, or players can kick it or slap it with their hands. They try to get the ball over a bar for one point or under the bar into a net for three points. Hurling is a very old sport and similar to modern rugby, soccer, field hockey, and football.

Bashi

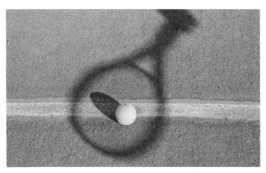

Bashi is a national sport in the Maldives, and only women play it. Between eight and eleven women play on a tennis court with tennis balls and one tennis racket. One player hits a ball with the racket on one side of the net, and players try to catch it on the other side. The woman who hits the ball faces away from the net and has to hit the ball backwards over her head! Women often get injured trying to catch the fast-moving balls with their bare hands.

B What sport do the activities describe? Check (✓) the answers.

	Capoeira	Hurling	Bashi
1. hit a ball backwards	☐	☐	☐
2. run very fast	☐	☐	☐
3. know what your opponent is thinking	☐	☐	☐
4. get a ball in a net	☐	☐	☐
5. move with music	☐	☐	☐
6. hit a ball over a net	☐	☐	☐

8 Choose the correct responses.

1. A: How often do you play golf, Monica?

   B: _Once a week._

     • I guess I'm OK.

     • Once a week.

     • About an hour.

2. A: How long do you spend on the golf course?

   B: _____

     • About four hours.

     • About average.

     • About three miles.

3. A: And how well do you play?

   B: _____

     • I'm not very well.

     • I almost never do.

     • I'm about average.

4. A: How good are you at other sports?

   B: _____

     • Not very good, actually.

     • I sometimes play twice a week.

     • Pretty well, I guess.

9 Look at the answers. Write questions using *how*.

1. A: _How long do you spend exercising?_

   B: I don't spend any time at all. In fact, I don't exercise.

2. A: _____ at playing football?

   B: I'm pretty good at it. I'm on the school team.

3. A: _____ for a walk?

   B: Almost every day. I really enjoy it.

4. A: _____

   B: Baseball? Pretty well, I guess. Yeah, I like it a lot.

5. A: _____

   B: I spend about an hour jogging.

10 Rewrite these sentences. Find another way to say each sentence using the words given.

1. I don't go bike riding very often.

   I hardly ever go bike riding._____ (hardly ever)

2. Tamara exercises twice a month.

   _____ (not very often)

3. Patty tries to keep fit.

   _____ (stay in shape)

4. Ricardo often exercises at the gym.

   _____ (work out)

5. I go jogging every day after work.

   _____ (always)

6. How good are you at tennis?

   _____ (play)

11 What do you think about fitness and sports? Answer these questions.

1. Do you like to exercise for a short time or a long time?

   _____

   _____

2. Do you prefer exercising in the morning or in the evening?

   _____

   _____

3. Which do you like better, walking or jogging?

   _____

   _____

4. Which do you like better, team sports or individual sports?

   _____

   _____

5. How good are you at sports like basketball and tennis?

   _____

   _____

6. What is a sport or game you don't like?

   _____

   _____

7 We went dancing!

1 Past tense

A Write the simple past of these regular verbs.

1. watch   _watched_
4. arrive   _____
7. travel   _____

2. play   _____
5. study   _____
8. wash   _____

3. invite   _____
6. hurry   _____
9. look   _____

B Write the simple present form of these irregular simple past verbs.

1.   _____eat_____ ate
5. _____ slept

2. _____ did
6. _____ spent

3. _____ met
7. _____ drove

4. _____ saw
8. _____ went

C Use two of the verbs above and write sentences about the past.

Example: _We saw the Eiffel Tower in Paris last year._

1. _____

2. _____

2 Use the cues to answer these questions.

1. Where did you go this weekend?

  I went to the zoo. _____ (to the zoo)

2. Who did you meet at the party?

_____ (a famous artist)

3. What did you buy?

_____ (a new pair of jeans)

4. How did you and Mario like the movie?

_____ (a lot)

5. Where did Faye and Bob spend their vacation?

_____ (in the country)

6. What time did you and Allison get home?

_____ (a little after 1:00)

3 What do you like to do alone? With other people? Complete the chart with activities from the box. Then add one more activity to each list.

	Activities I like to do alone	Activities I like to do with other people
cook dinner		
do homework		
exercise		
go shopping		
go to a sports event		
go to the movies		
have a picnic		
play video games		
take a vacation		
watch TV		

4 Complete the questions in this conversation.

A: How _did you spend the weekend_ ?

B: I spent the weekend with my sisters.

A: What _____?

B: Well, on Saturday, we went shopping.

A: That sounds like fun! What _____?

B: I bought a new pair of shoes and a new purse.

A: Where _____ on Sunday?

B: We went to an amusement park.

A: Oh, how _____?

B: We had a great time. In fact, we stayed there all day.

A: Really? What time _____?

B: We got home very late, around midnight.

5 Answer these questions with negative statements. Then add a positive statement using the information in the box.

- ☐ finish the project on Saturday
- ☐ go out with friends
- ☑ stay home all weekend
- ☐ take the bus
- ☐ watch it on TV
- ☐ work all day until six o'clock

1. **A:** Did you and John go to Anne's party on Saturday?

   B: _No, we didn't. We stayed home all weekend._

2. **A:** Beth left work at 2:00 yesterday afternoon. Did you go home early, too?

   B: _____

3. **A:** I watched TV all weekend. Did you spend the weekend at home, too?

   B: _____

4. **A:** I saw you and Amy at the library on Saturday. Did you work together on Sunday, too?

   B: _____

5. **A:** Giovanni drove me to work yesterday morning. Did you drive to work?

   B: _____

6. **A:** Sandy went to the baseball game last night. Did you and Martin go to the game?

   B: _____

6 Read about Pamela's week. Match the sentences that have a similar meaning.

A		B	
1. She was broke last week.	_f_	a. She had people over.	
2. She didn't work on Monday.	____	b. She did housework.	
3. She worked around the house.	____	c. She took the day off.	
4. She didn't wash the clothes.	____	d. She had a good time.	
5. She invited friends for dinner.	____	e. She didn't do the laundry.	
6. She had a lot of fun.	____	✓ f. She spent all her money.	

7 Did we take the same trip?

A Read the posts. Who went to Bangkok for the first time?

JOSEPH

We went to Thailand again for our summer vacation. We spent a week in Bangkok and did something every day. We went to the floating market very early one morning. We didn't buy anything there – we just looked. Another day, we went to Wat Phra Kaew, the famous Temple of the Emerald Buddha. Check out my pic!

Then we saw two more temples nearby. We also went on a river trip somewhere outside Bangkok. The best thing about the trip was the food. The next time we have friends over for dinner, I'm going to cook Thai food.

OLIVIA

Last summer, we spent our vacation in Thailand. We were very excited – it was our first trip there. We spent two days in Bangkok. Of course, we got a river taxi to the floating market. We bought some delicious fruit there. I'm posting a picture.

The next day we went to a very interesting temple called the Temple of the Emerald Buddha. We didn't have time to visit any other temples. However, we went to two historic cities – Ayutthaya and Sukhothai. Both have really interesting ruins. Everything was great. It's impossible to say what the best thing was about the trip.

B Who did these things on their trip? Check (✓) all correct answers.

	Joseph	Olivia
1. stayed for two days in Bangkok	☐	✓
2. visited the floating market	☐	☐
3. bought fruit	☐	☐
4. saw some historic ruins	☐	☐
5. traveled on the river	☐	☐
6. loved the food the most	☐	☐
7. enjoyed everything	☐	☐

8 Complete this conversation with *was*, *wasn't*, *were*, or *weren't*.

A: How _____was_____ your vacation in Thailand, Rich?

B: It _____ great. I really enjoyed it.

A: How long _____ you there?

B: We _____ there for two weeks.

A: _____ you in Bangkok the whole time?

B: No, we _____. We _____ in the mountains for a few days.

A: And how _____ the weather? _____ it good?

B: No, it _____ good at all! In fact, it _____ terrible. The city _____ very hot, and the mountains _____ cold and rainy!

9 Choose the correct questions to complete this conversation.

- ☐ And what was the best part?
- ☐ How long were you in Brazil?
- ☑ How was your vacation in South America?
- ☐ And how long were you in Argentina?
- ☐ How was the weather?

A: _How was your vacation in South America?_

B: It was a great trip. I really enjoyed Brazil and Argentina.

A: _____

B: I was in Brazil for ten days.

A: _____

B: For about eight days.

A: Wow, that's a long time! _____

B: It was hot and sunny the whole time.

A: _____

B: It was definitely the beaches in Brazil. Oh, and we learned the tango in Argentina!

Brazil

10 Complete the sentences with the correct words or phrases. Use the past tense when necessary.

1. We _____ a trip to Egypt last summer. (take / make / do)

2. My brothers _____ at home all weekend. (go dancing / play video games / take a bike ride)

3. I worked really hard in Germany last week. I was there _____. (in my car / on business / on vacation)

4. I'm sorry I was late. I had to _____ a phone call. (do / make / go)

5. I stayed home last night and _____ the laundry. (do / go / make)

11 My kind of vacation

A What do you like to do on vacation? Rank these activities from 1 (you like it the most) to 6 (you like it the least).

_____ go to the beach

_____ visit historical places

_____ go shopping

_____ visit museums

_____ spend time at home

_____ eat good food

B Answer these questions about vacations.

1. How often do you go on vacation?

   _____

2. How much time do you spend on vacation?

   _____

3. Who do you usually go with?

   _____

4. Where do you like to go?

   _____

5. What do you usually do on vacation?

   _____

8 How's the neighborhood?

1 Places

A Match the words in columns A and B. Write the names of the places.

A	B	
☑ coffee	☐ campus	**1.** _coffee shop_
☐ college	☑ shop	**2.**
☐ gas	☐ hotspot	**3.**
☐ grocery	☐ office	**4.**
☐ hair	☐ mall	**5.**
☐ movie	☐ salon	**6.**
☐ post	☐ station	**7.**
☐ shopping	☐ store	**8.**
☐ Wi-Fi	☐ theater	**9.**

B Write questions with *Is there a . . . ?* or *Are there any . . . ?* and the names of places from part A.

1. A: I need a haircut. _Is there a hair salon_____ near here?

   B: Yes, there's one on Grand Street.

2. A: I want to buy some new clothes. _____ near here?

   B: No, there isn't, but there's one in Center City.

3. A: I need to mail this package. _____ around here?

   B: Yes, there's one next to the bank.

4. A: I want to see a movie tonight. _____ around here?

   B: Yes, there's one in the shopping mall.

5. A: We need some gas. _____ on this street?

   B: No, there aren't, but there are a couple on Second Avenue.

6. A: We need to buy some cereal and some apples.

   _____ near here?

   B: Yes, there's one near the gym on Brown Street.

2 Look at these street maps of Springfield and Riverside. There are ten differences between them. Find the other eight.

> **Grammar note:** *There are; some and any*
>
> **Positive statement** | **Negative statement**
> There **are some** Wi-Fi hotspots near the bank. | There **aren't any** Wi-Fi hotspots near the bank.

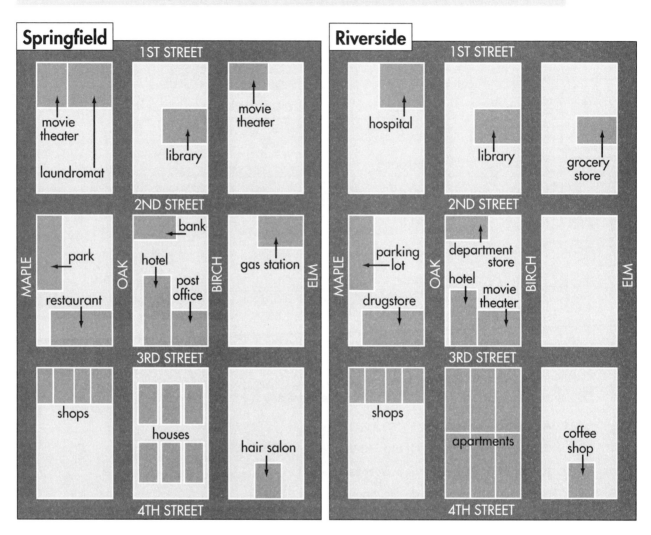

1. <u>There are some movie theaters on 1st Street in Springfield, but there aren't any in Riverside.</u>
2. <u>There's a park on the corner of 2nd Street and Maple in Springfield, but there isn't one in Riverside. There's a parking lot.</u>
3. _____
4. _____
5. _____
6. _____
7. _____
8. _____
9. _____
10. _____

3 Answer these questions. Use the map and the prepositions in the box.

☐ across from	☐ between	☐ in
☐ near	☑ next to	☐ on the corner of

1. Where's the nearest bank?

  <u>There's one next to the grocery store</u>
  <u>on 1st Avenue.</u>

2. Is there a post office near here?

  <u>Yes. There</u> _____

  _____

3. I'm looking for a drugstore.

  _____

  _____

4. Is there a laundromat in this neighborhood?

  _____

  _____

5. Is there a department store on River Street?

  _____

  _____

6. Are there any ATMs around here?

  _____

  _____

KING STREET

grocery store · hotel · ATM · bank · movie theater

PALM STREET

1ST AVENUE · drugstore · library · 2ND AVENUE · gas station · post office · 3RD AVENUE

LINCOLN STREET

laundromat · gym · department store · gym · hotel

RIVER STREET

4 Answer these questions about your city or neighborhood. Use the expressions in the box and your own information.

Yes, there is. There's one on . . .	Yes, there are. There are some on . . .
No, there isn't.	No, there aren't.

1. Are there any good coffee shops around the school? _____

  _____

2. Is there a drugstore near the school? _____

  _____

3. Are there any grocery stores in your neighborhood? _____

  _____

4. Is there a laundromat close to your home? _____

  _____

5 The grass is always greener

A Read the interviews. Where would Charles like to live? Where would Arlene like to live?

HOME | STORIES | PHOTOS

MODERN LIVING

WE ASKED TWO PEOPLE ABOUT THE PLACES THEY LIVE.

Charles Bell

"My neighborhood is very convenient — it's near the shopping center and the bus station. It's also safe. But those are the only good things about living downtown. It's very noisy because the streets are always full of people! The traffic is terrible, and parking is a big problem! I can never park on my own street. I'd like to live in a small town."

Arlene Miller

"My family and I live in a nice small town. It has a great square where people meet for social events, and there's music on summer evenings. It's a safe place to raise children. But there is no privacy here. Everyone in town knows what you are doing all the time. And I don't meet as many interesting people as when I lived in the city. It can be too quiet here. I want more action! I think it's better downtown."

♡ LIKE   💬 COMMENT

B How do Charles and Arlene feel about their neighborhoods? Complete the chart.

	Advantages	Disadvantages
Downtown	convenient	
Small Town		no privacy

C Do you think it's better to live downtown or in a small town? Why?

_____

_____

_____

D How do you feel about the place you live? Write about it.

_____

_____

_____

6 Complete the chart. Use words from the box.

☑ bank ☐ library ☐ people ☐ theater
☑ crime ☐ noise ☐ pollution ☐ traffic
☐ hospital ☐ parking ☐ school ☐ water

Count nouns		Noncount nouns	
bank		crime	

7 Write questions using *How much . . . ?* or *How many . . . ?* Then look at the picture and write answers to the questions. Use the expressions in the box.

☐ a few ☐ a lot ☐ many
☐ none ☐ not any ☑ only a little

1. trash   How much trash is there?   There's only a little.
2. buses
3. traffic
4. bicycles
5. police officers
6. crime

8 Choose the correct words or phrases to complete the conversation.

Andrea: Are there _____any_____ (any / one / none) coffee shops around here, Carlos?

Carlos: Sure. There are _____ (any / one / a lot). There's a coffee shop _____ (across from / between / on) the Daily Market, but it's expensive.

Andrea: Well, are there _____ (any / none / one) others?

Carlos: Yeah, there are _____ (a few / a little / one). There's a nice _____ (any / one / some) near here. It's called Morning Joe.

Andrea: That's perfect! Where is it, exactly?

Carlos: It's on Third Avenue, _____ (between / on / on the corner of) the National Bank and the Chinese restaurant.

Andrea: So let's go!

9 Choose the correct words or phrases.

1. I'm going to the grocery store to get some _____.
(clothes / gas / food)

2. We're taking a long drive. We need to stop at the _____.
(laundromat / gas station / drugstore)

3. I live on the 8th floor of my _____.
(apartment building / neighborhood / theater)

4. Our apartment is in the center of the city. We live _____.
(downtown / in the neighborhood / in the suburbs)

9 What does she look like?

1 Write the opposites. Use the words in the box.

☑ light ☐ straight ☐ young ☐ short ☐ tall

1. dark / _____light_____

2. curly / _____

3. short / _____

4. long / _____

5. elderly / _____

2 Descriptions

A Match the words in columns A and B. Write the descriptions.

A	B		
☑ medium	☐ aged	**1.**	*medium height*
☐ fairly	☐ brown	**2.**	
☐ good	☑ height	**3.**	
☐ middle	☐ long	**4.**	
☐ dark	☐ looking	**5.**	

B Answer the questions using the descriptions from part A.

1. A: How tall is he?

   B: _He's medium height._

2. A: What does he look like?

   B: _____

3. A: What color is his hair?

   B: _____

4. A: How long is his hair?

   B: _____

5. A: How old is he?

   B: _____

3 Complete this conversation with questions.

Marta: Let's find Arturo. I need to talk to him.

Alli: _What does he look like?_

Marta: He's very handsome, with curly brown hair.

Alli: And _____

Marta: It's medium length.

Alli: _____

Marta: He's fairly tall.

Alli: And _____

Marta: He's in his early twenties.

Alli: _____

Marta: Well, he usually wears jeans.

Alli: I think I see him over there. Is that him?

4 Describe yourself. How old are you? What do you look like? What are you wearing today?

_____

_____

_____

_____

_____

5 **Circle two things in each description that do not match the picture. Then correct the information.**

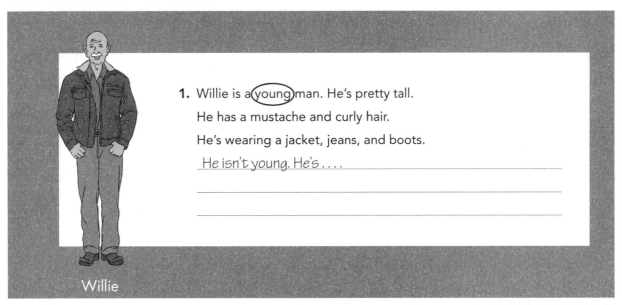

1. Willie is a (young) man. He's pretty tall.

   He has a mustache and curly hair.

   He's wearing a jacket, jeans, and boots.

   He isn't young. He's . . . .

   _____

   _____

Willie

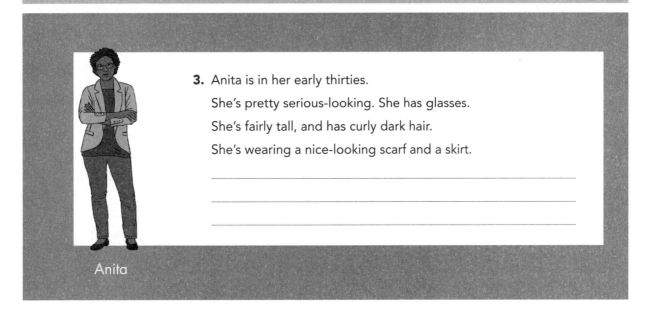

2. Sandy is about 25. She's very pretty.

   She's medium height. Her hair is long and blond.

   She's wearing a black sweater, a skirt, and sneakers.

   _____

   _____

   _____

Sandy

3. Anita is in her early thirties.

   She's pretty serious-looking. She has glasses.

   She's fairly tall, and has curly dark hair.

   She's wearing a nice-looking scarf and a skirt.

   _____

   _____

   _____

Anita

6 **Which of these clothing items are more formal? Which are more casual? Complete the chart.**

boots

cap

dress

high heels

jeans

jewelry

Formal	Casual
dress	

necktie

shirt

shorts

sneakers

suit

T-shirt

7 **Write a sentence about the people in the picture. Use the words in the box and participles.**

✓ man	☐ carry a jacket
☐ one	☐ wear sunglasses
☐ ones	✓ stand next to Angela
☐ short man	☐ talk to the man
☐ young woman	☐ wear a suit and tie

1. Brad is the man standing next to Angela.
2. _____
3. _____
4. _____
5. _____

Brad   Angela   Li Na   Matt   Tiffany   Rodrigo

8 Write sentences about the people in the picture. Use the words given.

1. _Charles and Natalie are the ones playing chess._ (ones / playing chess)
2. _____ (one / behind the couch)
3. _____ (ones / eating pizza)
4. _____ (woman / on the couch)
5. _____ (man / short black hair)

9 Rewrite the conversations. Find another way to say the sentences using the words in the box.

☑ near ☐ sitting ☐ wearing ☑ which ☐ who ☐ who

1. **A:** Who's Lucas?

   Which one's Lucas?

   B: He's the guy next to the window.

   He's the guy near the window.

2. **A:** Which ones are the servers?

   _____

   B: They're the ones in the red polo shirts.

   _____

3. **A:** Which one is Naomi?

   _____

   B: She's the one on the couch next to Lisa.

   _____

10 Which one is Jeff?

Complete Bill and Ruby's conversation at a party. Use the present continuous or the participle of the verbs in the box.

| ☐ cook | ☐ eat | ☑ look | ☐ play | ☐ sit | ☐ talk | ☐ use | ☐ wear |

Ruby: I'm glad you brought me to this party, Bill. I'm ____looking____ for someone here named Jeff.

Bill: Yeah, I don't know too many people here. But let's try to find him. Is he one of those guys _____ football? What about the guy with black hair and _____ the dark T-shirt?

Ruby: Hmm, no. That's not Jeff.

Bill: How about the one _____ the music system over there, in the white T-shirt.

Ruby: No, I know him. That's Ken.

Bill: Hmm. Oh, is that Jeff _____ at the table and _____ to the two women? It looks like they're already _____.

Ruby: No, not him, either. Gee, I wonder if Jeff even came to the party?

Bill: Well, he can't be the chef, right? The guy _____ vegetables at the grill?

Ruby: That's him! Hey, Jeff!

11 Choose the correct responses.

1. A: Who's Shawn?

   B: _The middle-aged man on the couch._

     • The middle-aged man on the couch.

     • That's right.

2. A: Where's Samantha?

   B: _____

     • She couldn't make it.

     • I'd like to meet her.

3. A: Is Avery the one wearing glasses?

   B: _____

     • That's right.

     • She's running late.

4. A: How tall is she?

   B: _____

     • Fairly long.

     • Pretty short.

10 Have you ever been there?

1 Match the verb forms in columns A and B.

	A		B
1.	make _g_	**a.**	tried
2.	ride ____	**b.**	eaten
3.	do ____	**c.**	seen
4.	eat ____	**d.**	had
5.	go ____	**e.**	ridden
6.	have ____	**f.**	heard
7.	be ____	✓ **g.**	made
8.	hear ____	**h.**	done
9.	see ____	**i.**	gone
10.	try ____	**j.**	been

2 Complete the questions in these conversations. Use the present perfect of the verbs in Exercise 1.

1. **A:** _____Have you seen_____ Al's new dog?

   B: Yes, it's so cute!

2. **A:** How many times _____
   to the gym this month?

   B: Actually, not at all. Let's go later today!

3. **A:** How many phone calls _____
   today?

   B: I made two calls – both to you!

4. **A:** _____ your homework yet?

   B: Yes, I have. I did it after class.

5. **A:** _____ at the new Italian
   restaurant?

   B: Yes, we already have. It's very good but a
   little expensive.

6. **A:** How long _____
   those boots?

   B: I bought them on Monday.

3 *Already* and *yet*

A Check (✓) the things you've already done. Put an ✗ next to the things you haven't done yet.

1. _____ graduated from high school   4. _____ been in an airplane
2. _____ gotten married   5. _____ learned to drive
3. _____ ridden a horse   6. _____ traveled abroad

B Write sentences about each activity in part A. Use *already* and *yet*.

> **Grammar note:** *Already* and *yet*
>
> ***Already*** **is used in positive statements with the present perfect.**
> I've **already** graduated from high school.
> ***Yet*** **is used in negative statements with the present perfect.**
> I haven't gotten married **yet**.

1. _____   4. _____
   _____   _____

2. _____   5. _____
   _____   _____

3. _____   6. _____
   _____   _____

4 Complete these sentences with *for* or *since*.

1. Jill has driven the same car _____*since*_____ 2004.
2. I have been a teacher _____ several years.
3. I haven't had this much fun _____ I was a kid!
4. I'm so sleepy. I've been awake _____ 4:00 this morning.
5. Kyoko was an exchange student in Peru _____ a whole semester.
6. Marcus has lived in Dubai _____ 2010.
7. How are you? I haven't seen you _____ high school.
8. Where have you been? I've been here _____ over an hour!
9. Mr. and Mrs. Lopez have been married _____ nearly 50 years.

5 Look at these pictures. How often have you done these things? Write sentences
using the expressions in the box.

I've . . . many times.	I've . . . once or twice.
I've . . . three or four times.	I haven't . . . lately.
I've . . . several times.	I've never . . .

eat Thai food

go to a concert

1. _____

_____

2. _____

_____

go skiing

play an instrument

3. _____

_____

4. _____

_____

see an opera

play golf

5. _____

_____

6. _____

_____

6 Lost tales

A Read the two blog posts. Where did each blogger go? What activity did each one want to do?

NO WAY OUT!

Have you ever visited Mexico? If so, then you know it is famous for its Aztec ruins. Last summer my Spanish class visited Mexico City. We went on a tour of Aztec ruins that are found under the city's main square. We walked for two hours underground in the dark halls. It was like being in a cave. There are many interesting things to see. I wanted to get a better look at a statue, so I went around some ropes that are supposed to keep tourists out. Several minutes later, I came out on the other side, but my group disappeared! I couldn't hear any voices, and I didn't know which way to go. I was too embarrassed to shout, so I wandered around the halls trying to find my group. I started to get nervous. It seemed like I was alone for hours. I walked around in the darkness until I finally heard the professor calling my name. He was very worried, and I was relieved! For the rest of our trip in Mexico, he made sure I never left his sight. My friends still call me "Cave Woman."

NO WAY IN!

I have been to Europe many times but never to Greece until last summer. It was an unforgettable experience! I was staying at a small hotel in Athens. It was in a part of town where most tourists don't stay, but it was cheaper there, and I wanted to practice speaking Greek with people. One evening I went for a walk before dinner. Soon it started to get dark. I didn't want to get lost, and I remembered I had a small map of Athens in my wallet. My wallet! It wasn't in my pocket. I thought, "I've left it in the hotel room . . . and my hotel key is in my wallet!" It took me a long time to get back to the hotel, but I made it. The door was locked, of course. Sometimes I talk to myself when I'm upset. Well, I must have said out loud, "I've lost my wallet, I've locked myself out, and I've missed dinner!" Just then, the hotel manager appeared. I guess he heard me talking. He said something in Greek and pointed to his house. I followed him. He and his family were having a big Greek dinner. They wanted me to join them. The manager eventually let me into my room. But first, I ate one of the best meals I've ever had. And forgetting my wallet was the best mistake I've ever made!

B In which story or stories did the writer(s) do these things? Write *1*, *2*, or *1 and 2*.

____1____ went to ruins	_____ stayed at a hotel
_____ went to a foreign country	_____ went underground
_____ got lost	_____ made a mistake
_____ got help from someone	_____ went on the trip alone

C Write about an adventure you have had. What happened? What went wrong?

_____

_____

_____

_____

7 Look at the answers. Write questions using *Have you ever . . . ?*

text messaging

rugby match

sushi

Houston

1. **A:** _Have you ever sent a text message during class?_

   B: No, I've never sent a text message during class.

2. **A:** _____

   B: Actually, I saw a rugby match last week on TV. It was awesome!

3. **A:** _____

   B: Yes, I love sushi.

4. **A:** _____

   B: No, I haven't. But my uncle lives in Houston.

5. **A:** _____

   B: Yes, I visited an amusement park last month.

6. **A:** _____

   B: No, I haven't. I don't think I would like camping.

7. **A:** _____

   B: Yes, I have. I once rode my aunt's motorcycle.

8 Write your own answers to the questions (speaker A) in Exercise 7. Use expressions like the ones from the list.

Yes, I have.	I . . . yesterday.	No, I haven't.	I've never . . .
	I . . . on Monday.		I . . . yet.
	I . . . last year.		
	I . . . in August.		

1. _____
2. _____
3. _____
4. _____
5. _____
6. _____
7. _____

9 Complete the conversation. Use the simple past or the present perfect of the words given.

A: ___Have___ you ever ___lost___ (lose) anything valuable?

B: Yes, I _____ (lose) my cell phone last month.

A: _____ you _____ (find) it yet?

B: No. Actually, I _____ already _____ (buy) a new one. Look!

A: Oh, that's nice. Where _____ you _____ (buy) it?

B: I _____ (get) it at the mall last weekend. What about you? _____ you ever _____ (lose) anything valuable?

A: Well, I _____ (leave) my leather jacket in a coffee shop a couple of months ago.

B: Oh, no! _____ you _____ (go) back and look for it?

A: Well, I _____ (call) them, but it was gone.

10 Choose the correct responses.

1. A: Has John visited his brother lately?
   B: ___No, he hasn't.___
   - How many times?
   - No, he hasn't.

2. A: Are you having a good time?
   B: _____
   - Yes, in a long time.
   - Yes, really good.

3. A: How long did Theresa stay at the party?
   B: _____
   - For two hours.
   - Since midnight.

4. A: Have you had breakfast?
   B: _____
   - Yes, in a few minutes.
   - Yes, I've already eaten.

5. A: How many times has Tony lost his keys?
   B: _____
   - Twice.
   - Not yet.

6. A: Do you want to see that new movie?
   B: _____
   - I never have. What about you?
   - Sure. I hear it's great.

7. A: Have you been here long?
   B: _____
   - No, not yet.
   - No, just a few minutes.

8. A: Have you seen Sara today?
   B: _____
   - Yes, I saw her this morning.
   - Yes, tomorrow.

11 It's a really nice city.

1 Choose the correct words to complete the sentences.

Singapore

Chicago

1. Prices are high in Singapore. Everything is very ___expensive___ there.
   (cheap / expensive / noisy)

2. Chicago has amazing skyscrapers right next to a gorgeous lake. It's a really _____ city.
   (beautiful / cheap / quiet)

3. My hometown is not an exciting place. The nightlife there is pretty _____.
   (boring / nice / interesting)

4. Some parts of our city are fairly dangerous. It's not very _____ late at night.
   (hot / interesting / safe)

5. The streets in this city are always full of people, cars, and buses. It's a very _____ city.
   (spacious / crowded / relaxing)

2 Choose the correct questions to complete this conversation.

- ☐ What's the weather like?
- ☐ Is it big?
- ☐ Is the nightlife exciting?
- ☑ What's your hometown like?

A: _What's your hometown like?_

B: My hometown? It's a pretty nice place, and the people are very friendly.

A: _____

B: No, it's fairly small, but it's not too small.

A: _____

B: The winter is wet and really cold. It's very nice in the summer, though.

A: _____

B: No! It's really boring. There are no good restaurants or nightclubs.

3 Choose the correct conjunctions and rewrite the sentences.

Grammar note: *And, but, though,* and *however*

Use *and* for additional information.
It's an exciting city, **and** the weather is great.
Use *but, though,* and *however* for contrasting information.
It's very safe during the day, **but** it's pretty dangerous at night.
The summers are hot. The evenings are fairly cold, **though**.
It is a fairly large city. It's not too interesting, **however**.

Colorado

Dubai

Hong Kong

1. Colorado is beautiful in the summer. It's a great place to go hiking. (and / but)

Colorado is beautiful in the summer, and it's a great place to go hiking.

2. Dubai is a very nice place. The summers are terribly hot. (and / though)

3. Hong Kong is an exciting city. It's a fun place to sightsee. (and / however)

4. My hometown has some great restaurants. It's not a good place for shopping. (and / but)

5. Our hometown is somewhat ugly. It has some beautiful old homes. (and / however)

4 Check (✓) if these sentences need *a* or *an*. Then write *a* or *an* in the correct places.

> **Grammar note: A and *an***
>
> **Use *a* or *an* with (adverb +) adjective + singular noun.**
> It has **a fairly new park**. It's **an old city**.
> **Don't use *a* or *an* with (adverb +) adjective.**
> It's **fairly new**. It's **old**.

1. ✓ London has ⌄very famous Ferris wheel. *(a)*
2. ☐ Restaurants are very cheap in Ecuador.
3. ☐ Brisbane is clean city.
4. ☐ The buildings in Florence are really beautiful.
5. ☐ Apartments are very expensive in Hong Kong.
6. ☐ Sapporo is very cold city in the winter.
7. ☐ Beijing's museums are really excellent.
8. ☐ Mumbai is exciting place to visit.

5 Complete the description of Paris with *is* or *has*.

PARIS: City of Light

Paris _____ France's biggest city. It _____ a very lively city with an interesting history. It _____ a city of interesting buildings and churches, and it _____ many beautiful parks. It also _____ some of the best museums in the world. Paris _____ nice weather most of the year, but it _____ pretty cold in the winter. It _____ a popular city with foreign tourists and _____ millions of visitors a year. The city _____ famous for its fashion and _____ many excellent stores. Paris _____ convenient trains and buses that cross the city, so it _____ easy for tourists to get around.

It's a really nice city. **63**

A Scan the webpage. Where is each city?

SEOUL

Seoul was founded in 18 BCE. It is South Korea's capital and today has a population of 10.5 million people. Seoul is famous for producing popular music and films that are very well known in Asia, Latin America, and the Middle East. The city is surrounded by mountains and located on the Han River. It has an excellent transportation system that can take you to 115 museums, monuments, parks, and music festivals throughout the city. The best time to visit Seoul is in the fall and the spring. Winters can be quite cold and summers very hot.

QUITO

Quito sits 2,850 meters above sea level and is the highest capital city in the world. Its population is 2.6 million people. The city is located near the equator in the country of Ecuador (which means "equator" in Spanish). Quito's downtown center, one of the most beautiful in the Americas, has not changed much since the Spanish founded the city in 1534. On a day trip from Quito, you can go walking in the mountains and visit a volcano there. Because of the city's elevation and location on the equator, the weather there is pleasant all year.

RABAT

Rabat is located on the Atlantic Ocean. It was founded in 1146. Although Rabat is the capital of Morocco, its population is only about 580,000 people. The weather is cool at night with hot days in the summer and mild days in the winter. Mawazine, a famous world music festival, takes place in Rabat in the spring. You can visit the Kasbah, an old fortress, and enjoy the architecture, gardens, and the view of the ocean. Rabat's outdoor markets sell beautiful handmade goods. Explore the city and enjoy a delicious Moroccan meal!

B Read the webpage and complete the chart.

City	Date founded	Population	Attractions
Seoul			
Quito			
Rabat			

C Complete the sentences.

1. _____ and _____ have music festivals.

2. _____ is the capital city with the smallest population.

3. _____ is the oldest capital city.

4. _____ has the capital city with the highest altitude.

7 Complete the sentences. Use phrases from the box.

- ☐ shouldn't miss
- ☐ can take
- ✓ should see
- ☐ shouldn't stay
- ☐ can get
- ☐ shouldn't walk

1. You _____ should see _____ the new zoo. It's very interesting.

2. You _____ near the airport. It's too noisy.

3. You _____ the museum. It has some new exhibits.

4. You _____ a bus tour of the city if you like.

5. You _____ alone at night. It's too dangerous.

6. You _____ a taxi if you're out late.

8 Complete the conversation with *should* or *shouldn't* and *I* or *you*.

A: I'm taking my vacation in Japan. What _____ should I _____ do there?

B: _____ miss Kyoto, the old capital city. There are a lot of beautiful old buildings. For example, _____ see the Ryoanji Temple.

A: Sounds great. Hakone is very popular, too. _____ go there?

B: Yes, _____. It's very interesting, and the hot springs are fantastic.

A: _____ take a lot of money with me?

B: No, _____. You can use the ATMs in Japan.

A: So when _____ go there?

B: In the spring or the fall. You can see the cherry blossoms or the fall colors.

9 Ask questions about a place you want to visit. Use *can*, *should*, or *shouldn't*.

1. the time to visit

   What time of year should I visit?

2. things to see and do there

   _____

3. things not to do

   _____

4. special foods to try

   _____

5. fun things to buy

   _____

6. other interesting things to do

   _____

10 Rewrite the sentences. Think of another way to express each sentence using the words given.

1. It's a polluted city.

   It isn't a clean city. _____ (not clean)

2. You really should visit the new aquarium.

   _____ (not miss)

3. Apartments are not cheap in my country.

   _____ (extremely expensive)

4. This neighborhood is not noisy at all.

   _____ (very quiet)

5. When should we visit the city?

   _____ (a good time)

12 It's important to get rest.

1 Any suggestions?

A Check (✓) the best advice for each health problem.

1. a backache
- ✓ use a heating pad
- ☐ get some exercise
- ☐ drink herbal tea

2. a bad cold
- ☐ see a dentist
- ☐ go to bed and rest
- ☐ go swimming

3. a burn
- ☐ take a multivitamin
- ☐ put it under cold water
- ☐ drink warm milk

4. a headache
- ☐ take some vitamin C
- ☐ take some pain medicine
- ☐ take a cough drop

5. an insect bite
- ☐ apply anti-itch cream
- ☐ use eyedrops
- ☐ drink lots of liquids

6. sore muscles
- ☐ drink lots of hot water
- ☐ take some cold medicine
- ☐ use some ointment

B Write a question about each problem in part A. Then write answers using the words from the box. Use the advice in part A or your own ideas.

| It's important . . . | It's sometimes helpful . . . | It's a good idea . . . |

1. A: _What should you do for a backache?_
   B: _It's sometimes helpful to use a heating pad._
2. A: _____
   B: _____
3. A: _____
   B: _____
4. A: _____
   B: _____
5. A: _____
   B: _____
6. A: _____
   B: _____

2 **Rewrite these sentences. Give advice using** *it's important . . . ,* *it's a good idea . . . ,* **or** *it's sometimes helpful . . . .*

Grammar note: Negative infinitives		
Problem	**Advice**	**Negative infinitive**
For the flu,	don't exercise a lot.	For the flu, it's a good idea **not to exercise** a lot.

1. For a toothache, don't eat cold foods.

   For a toothache, it's important not to eat cold foods.

2. For a sore throat, don't talk too much.

   _____

3. For a burn, don't put ice on it.

   _____

4. For insomnia, don't drink coffee at night.

   _____

5. For a fever, don't get out of bed.

   _____

3 **Check (✓) three health problems you have had. Write what you did for each one. Use the remedies below or your own remedies.**

Health problems

☐ a cough   ☐ a backache

☐ a headache   ☐ the hiccups

☐ insomnia   ☐ a sunburn

☐ a cold   ☐ stress

Some remedies

take some pain medicine

get some medicine from the drugstore

use some lotion

put some ointment on it

take some cough drops

see my doctor/dentist

go to bed

do nothing

Example: _Yesterday, I had a bad headache, so I took some pain medicine._

1. _____

2. _____

3. _____

4 Learning to laugh

A Scan the article. Check (✓) the sentence that is the better summary of the article.

☐ People who laugh at least once a day live longer than people who don't.
☐ Laughter has important health benefits for your body.

LAUGH IT OFF

Have you laughed today? If so, you probably did a good thing for your health.

Psychologists now consider laughing to be an important practice for good health. Laughter is known to reduce stress, improve the body's ability to fight disease, and make life happier and more interesting. It adds to the pleasure we get from other people and the enjoyment other people get from us.

Dr. Madan Kataria, the founder of Laughter Yoga, discovered that laughter does not have to be real to be good for the body. In Laughter Yoga, people combine yoga breathing with laughter exercises in a group. This allows people to practice laughing without the presence of humor.

Dr. Kataria has found that the body responds well just to the physical act of laughing.

Dr. Annette Goodheart was one of the first doctors in the U.S. to promote laughter for health. In her book *Laughter Therapy: How to Laugh About Everything in Your Life That is Not Really Funny*, she writes, "Everyone usually knows what they think is funny or can laugh at. But I help people laugh about things that aren't funny and support them in re-balancing and resolving their pain."

People who say that laughter is the best medicine might be right. A laugh a day keeps the doctor away!

B Check (✓) True or False.

	True	False
1. Laughter can help the body fight disease.	☐	☐
2. The more you laugh, the more other people like you.	☐	☐
3. Laughter is healthier for you if it is real.	☐	☐
4. Psychologists believe it is healthy to laugh at all situations.	☐	☐
5. Dr. Goodheart helped patients focus only on funny things.	☐	☐

C Describe a time you laughed hard at something. How did you feel afterward?

_____

_____

_____

5 What do you suggest?

A Complete the word map with medicines from the list.

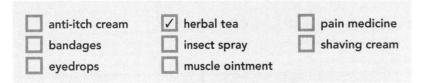

☐ anti-itch cream	☑ herbal tea	☐ pain medicine
☐ bandages	☐ insect spray	☐ shaving cream
☐ eyedrops	☐ muscle ointment	

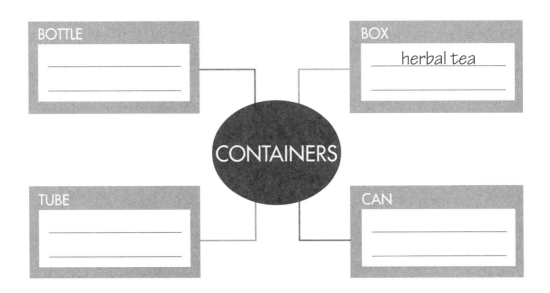

BOTTLE
_____
_____

BOX
___herbal tea___
_____

CONTAINERS

TUBE
_____
_____

CAN
_____
_____

B What should these people buy? Give advice. Use the containers and medicine from part A.

1. Danielle is having trouble sleeping.

    She should buy a box of herbal tea.

2. Simon has a bad headache.

    _____

3. Maria's shoulders are sore after her workout.

    _____

4. There may be mosquitoes where Brenda's camping.

    _____

5. Sam has a cut on his hand.

    _____

6. Graciela has dry, itchy skin on her feet.

    _____

7. Nathan cut his chin when he shaved with soap and water.

    _____

8. Sally's eyes are red and itchy.

    _____

6 Check (✓) the correct sentences to make conversations.

1. **Pharmacist:** ☑ Can I help you?

   ☐ Should I help you?

   Customer: ☐ Yes. Can I have a bottle of pain medicine?

   ☐ Yes. I suggest a bottle of pain medicine.

   Pharmacist: Here you are.

   Customer: ☐ And what do you need for a sunburn?

   ☐ And what do you have for a sunburn?

   Pharmacist: ☐ Do you suggest this lotion?

   ☐ I suggest this lotion.

   Customer: Thanks.

2. **Pharmacist:** Hi. Can I help you?

   Customer: ☐ Yes. Can I suggest something for sore muscles?

   ☐ Yes. Could I have something for sore muscles?

   Pharmacist: ☐ Sure. Try this ointment.

   ☐ Sure. Could I try this ointment?

   Customer: ☐ Thanks. And what should you get for the flu?

   ☐ Thanks. And what do you suggest for the flu?

   Pharmacist: ☐ Can I have some of these tablets? They really work.

   ☐ Try some of these tablets. They really work.

   Customer: ☐ OK, thanks. I'll take them. And you should get a box of tissues.

   ☐ OK, thanks. I'll take them. And could I have a box of tissues?

   Pharmacist: Sure. Here you are.

7 Complete this conversation with the correct words.

A: Wow, you don't look very good! Do you feel OK?

B: No, I think I'm getting a cold. What should I do _____ it?
                                                                    (for / to / with)

A: You should stay _____ home and go _____ bed.
                                 (at / in / of)   (in / of / to)

B: You're probably right. I've got a really bad cough, too.

A: Try drinking some hot tea _____ honey. It really helps.
                                       (for / of / with)

B: Anything else?

A: Yeah, I suggest you get a big box _____ tissues!
                                                    (at / in / of)

8 Give suggestions for these problems. Use words from the box.

> Try . . .   I suggest . . .   You should . . .

1. I can't stop sneezing.

   Try some allergy medicine. _____

2. I have a stomachache.

_____

3. I don't have any energy.

_____

4. I think I'm getting a cold.

_____

5. I'm stressed out!

_____

6. I have a very sore throat.

_____

13 What would you like?

1 **Show that you agree. Write sentences with the words given.**

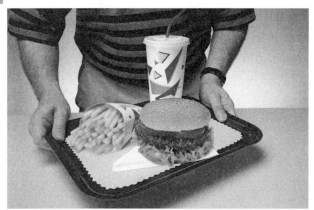

1. A: I don't want fast food tonight.

    B: _I don't either._ (either)

2. A: I really like Mexican food.

    B: _____ (so)

3. A: I'm in the mood for Italian food.

    B: _____ (too)

4. A: I can't stand spicy food.

    B: _____ (neither)

5. A: I don't like greasy food very much.

    B: _____ (either)

6. A: I want to eat healthy food for lunch.

    B: _____ (too)

2 What do you think?

A Look at the pictures. Write sentences about the food. Use the expressions in the box and the given words.

Useful expressions

I love . . .	I'm crazy about . . .
I can't stand . . .	I'm not crazy about . . .
I don't like . . . very much.	It's a little too . . .
I like . . . a lot.	

greasy

1. It's a little too greasy.

bland

2. _____

rich

3. _____

salty

4. _____

healthy

5. _____

B What are three of your favorite kinds of food? Write what you like about them.

_____
_____
_____
_____

3 To your taste

A Skim the restaurant reviews. Match the reviewer with the number of stars.

1. Carlota   ★   Awful!
2. Adam   ★ ★ ★   Pretty good.
3. Luka   ★ ★ ★ ★ ★   Fantastic!!

YUM! Restaurant Reviews   Find a restaurant ...

QUINOA CORNER
175 PLEASANT ST.

Carlota

Quinoa Corner is my latest discovery! This international food restaurant has everything: delicious steak, hamburgers, Mexican enchiladas, Mediterranean salads, and vegetarian and vegan dishes, too. When I was there last Saturday, I ordered a grilled salmon with baby asparagus and a baked potato. Delicious! And the atmosphere is wonderful. The servers are dressed as cowboys and cowgirls. Every hour they do a square dance and sing a song for the diners. I love this place!

Luka

Last Sunday I took my wife to Quinoa Corner. I had sushi with rice and a cucumber salad. My wife had lamb curry with spicy vegetables and garlic bread. For dessert we both had chocolate cake. The sushi was quite good, although the salad was not as fresh as I'd like. My wife said that her curry was delicious, but that the vegetables were a little too salty. And I thought the servers were kind of silly. Despite those problems, we still recommend this restaurant.

Adam

For dinner last Thursday, I visited Quinoa Corner for the first time. I ordered the quinoa burger and an almond milkshake. They served me a real hamburger! While I was trying to explain the mistake to my server, she stepped away and began to dance and sing with the other "cowboys"! It took another half hour before my quinoa burger got to the table. When it did, it was cold, bland, and greasy! I do not recommend this restaurant.

B Read the reviews and complete the chart.

	Carlota	Luka	Luka's wife	Adam
Ordered:				
Problems:	☐ yes ☐ no	☐ yes ☐ no	☐ yes ☐ no	☐ yes ☐ no
Recommends:	☐ yes ☐ no	☐ yes ☐ no	☐ yes ☐ no	☐ yes ☐ no

4 Check (✓) the item that does not belong in each group.

1. ☐ apples
   ☑ broccoli
   ☐ strawberries

2. ☐ sushi
   ☐ pasta
   ☐ bread

3. ☐ ice cream
   ☐ iced coffee
   ☐ iced tea

4. ☐ corn
   ☐ green beans
   ☐ pork

5. ☐ beef
   ☐ bread
   ☐ chicken

6. ☐ a cookie
   ☐ a turkey sandwich
   ☐ a hamburger

5 Use one or more words to complete this conversation between a server and a customer.

Server: May I take your order?

Customer: _____Yes, I'll have_____ the salmon.

Server: What kind of dressing _____ on your salad – French, blue cheese, or vinaigrette?

Customer: _____ like French, please.

Server: And would you like _____ to drink?

Customer: Yes, _____ have iced coffee.

Server: With milk and sugar?

Customer: Yes, _____.

Server: Anything else?

Customer: No, _____. That'll _____ all.

6 Choose the correct responses.

1. A: What would you like?

    B: _I'll have a beef burrito._

- I'll be your server today.
- Yes, I'd like to.
- I'll have a beef burrito.

2. A: Would you like soup or salad?

    B: _____

- I guess I will, thanks.
- I'd like soup, please.
- Yes, please.

3. A: What would you like on your pizza?

    B: _____

- I'll have pepperoni.
- I'd like a soda, please.
- Small, please.

4. A: Would you like anything to drink?

    B: _____

- No, thanks.
- Yes, a hamburger, please.
- I'll have some noodles, please.

5. A: What flavor ice cream would you like?

    B: _____

- Fresh, please.
- Vanilla, please.
- Ice cream, please.

6. A: Would you like anything else?

    B: _____

- Yes, thank you very much.
- Not at all, thanks.
- That'll be all, thanks.

7 Choose the correct words.

1. Baked potatoes are less _____greasy_____ than french fries. (greasy / healthy / spicy)

2. In a restaurant, the server takes your _____. (table / order / service)

3. Many people like _____ on their salad. (dessert / dressing / soda)

4. Some people rarely cook with spices. They prefer food to be _____. (bland / hot / rich)

5. Strawberry is a popular ice cream _____. (drink / flavor / meal)

8 Complete the conversation. Use the words and expressions in the box.

- ☐ am
- ☐ can
- ☐ can't stand them
- ☐ do
- ☐ favorite kind of food
- ☐ like it a lot
- ✓ neither
- ☐ so
- ☐ too
- ☐ I'll
- ☐ would

Maria: I feel tired tonight. I really don't want to cook.

Courtney: _____Neither_____ do I. Let's order out. Do you like Chinese food?

Maria: It's delicious! I _____!

Courtney: I do, _____. It's my _____.
Let's call Beijing Express for home delivery.

Maria: Great idea! Their food is always good. I eat there a lot.

Courtney: _____ do I. Well, what _____ you like tonight?

Maria: I'm in the mood for some soup.

Courtney: So _____ I. And I think _____ have orange chicken
and fried rice.

Maria: OK, let's order. Oh, wait. They don't take credit cards, and I don't have any cash on me.

Courtney: Neither _____ I. Too bad! What should we do?

Maria: Well, let's look in the refrigerator. Hmm. Do you like boiled eggs?

Courtney: I _____!

Maria: Actually, neither _____ I.

14 It's the coldest city!

1 Geography

A Circle the correct word.

1. This is a mountain with a hole on top. Smoke and lava sometimes come out, and it can be dangerous.
   - **a.** waterfall
   - **(b.)** volcano
   - **c.** hill

2. This is a dry, sandy place. It doesn't rain much here, and there aren't many plants.
   - **a.** desert
   - **b.** sea
   - **c.** volcano

3. This is a low area of land between mountains or hills.
   - **a.** island
   - **b.** valley
   - **c.** beach

4. This is an area of water with land all around it.
   - **a.** hill
   - **b.** island
   - **c.** lake

5. This is a flow of water that happens when a river falls from a high place.
   - **a.** hill
   - **b.** canyon
   - **c.** waterfall

6. This is a large area of land that has lots of trees on it.
   - **a.** desert
   - **b.** forest
   - **c.** river

B Complete the names. Use words from the box.

☐ Canyon	☐ Falls	☐ Ocean	☑ Lake
☐ Desert	☐ Mount	☐ River	☐ Sea

1. _____Lake_____ Superior
2. Amazon _____
3. Grand _____
4. Atlantic _____
5. Mojave _____
6. Niagara _____
7. Mediterranean _____
8. _____ Everest

2 Write the comparative and superlative forms of the words given.

Spelling note: Comparatives and superlatives			
	Adjective	**Comparative**	**Superlative**
Add *-er* or *-est* to most words.	long	long**er**	the long**est**
Add *-r* or *-st* to words ending in *-e*.	large	larg**er**	the larg**est**
Drop the y and add *-ier* or *-iest*.	dry	dr**ier**	the dr**iest**
Double the final consonant and add *-er* or *-est*.	big	bi**gger**	the bi**ggest**

1. busy   _busier_   _the busiest_
2. cool   _____ _____
3. friendly   _____ _____
4. heavy   _____ _____
5. nice   _____ _____

6. noisy   _____ _____
7. old   _____ _____
8. safe   _____ _____
9. small   _____ _____
10. wet   _____ _____

3 Complete this conversation. Use the superlative form of the words given.

Keegan: So where did you go for your vacation, Kathy?

Kathy: Japan.

Keegan: How exciting! Did you have a good time?

Kathy: It was terrific! I think Japan is ___ _the most exciting_ ___ (exciting) country in Asia.

Keegan: Well, it certainly has some of _____ (interesting) cities in the world – Tokyo, Osaka, and Kyoto.

Kathy: Yeah. I had _____ (good) time in Kyoto. It's _____ (beautiful) city I've ever seen. Of course, it's also one of _____ (popular) tourist attractions. It was _____ (crowded) city I visited this summer.

Keegan: I've always wanted to visit Japan. What's it like in the winter?

Kathy: Actually, I think that's _____ (bad) time to visit because I don't like cold weather. However, I think the Sapporo Snow Festival is _____ (fascinating) festival in the world.

4 Complete these sentences. Use the comparative or the superlative form of the words given.

Badwater Basin

the Suez Canal

Mount Waialeale

1. Badwater Basin in California's Death Valley is _____the lowest_____ (low) point in North America.

2. The Suez Canal joins the Mediterranean and Red Seas. It is 190 kilometers (118 miles) long. It is _____longer than_____ (long) the Panama Canal.

3. Mount Waialeale in Hawaii gets 1,170 centimeters (460 inches) of rain a year. It is _____ (wet) place on Earth!

4. Canada and Russia are _____ (large) countries in the world.

5. Russia is _____ (large) Canada.

6. _____ (high) waterfall in the world is in Venezuela.

7. The Atacama Desert in Chile is _____ (dry) place in the world.

8. _____ (hot) capital city in the world is Muscat, Oman.

9. The continent of Antarctica is _____ (cold) any other place in the world.

10. The Himalayas are some of _____ (dangerous) mountains to climb.

11. Mont Blanc in the French Alps is _____ (high) the Matterhorn in the Swiss Alps.

12. The Pacific Ocean is _____ (deep) the Atlantic Ocean. At one place, the Pacific Ocean is 11,033 meters (36,198 feet) deep.

5 The coldest and the windiest!

A Scan the article about Antarctica. In what ways is it different from other places on Earth? Why do scientists work there?

ANTARCTICA is the most southern continent in the world. It's like nowhere else on Earth. It's much larger than Europe and nearly twice the size of Australia. It's an icy plateau with the South Pole at its center. Antarctica is the coldest and windiest place in the world, even colder and windier than the North Pole. Although 98 percent of Antarctica is covered in ice, it is considered a desert. Along the coast, annual precipitation is only 200 millimeters (eight inches) a year. Very few plants grow there, but there is some wildlife, including whales, seals, and penguins. In the summer, the sun shines for 24 hours a day, but in the winter, it's completely dark for about three months.

When Captain James Cook sailed around the continent in the 1770s, he found no one living there. Today, a few scientists work in Antarctica, but they only spend fairly short periods of time there. Many of these scientists live and work on the Antarctic Peninsula. This area is the closest part of Antarctica to South America, the continent's nearest neighbor. Many of these scientists are studying the effects of climate change there. Antarctica has warmed by about 2.5 degrees Celsius since 1950. Some ice is melting in certain parts of the continent. However, unlike the vast melting that is happening in the Arctic, the ice in Antarctica is actually growing in spite of global warming.

Scientists think that this cold and lonely place can teach us a lot about the earth and how to keep it safe.

B Read about Antarctica. Check (✓) True or False.

	True	False
1. Antarctica is bigger than Europe.	☐	☐
2. The North Pole is the coldest place in the world.	☐	☐
3. The coasts in Antarctica get a lot of snow.	☐	☐
4. In Antarctica, it never gets dark in the summer.	☐	☐
5. Captain Cook discovered a few people living in Antarctica.	☐	☐
6. The Antarctic Peninsula is the closest part of Antarctica to South America.	☐	☐
7. Ice in Antarctica is melting throughout the continent.	☐	☐

6 Geography quiz

Use the words in the box. Write questions about the pictures. Then circle the correct answers.

<table>
<tr><td>☐ How big</td><td>☐ How deep</td><td>☐ How long</td></tr>
<tr><td>☐ How cold</td><td>☐ How far</td><td>☑ How high</td></tr>
</table>

Angel Falls

1. <u>How high is Angel Falls?</u>
   a. It's 979 meters (3,212 feet) tall.
   (b.) It's 979 meters high.

the Yangtze River

2. _____
   a. It's 6,300 kilometers (3,917 miles) long.
   b. It's 6,300 kilometers high.

Antarctica

3. _____
   a. It gets up to –88.3 degrees Celsius (–126.9 degrees Fahrenheit).
   b. It gets down to –88.3 degrees Celsius.

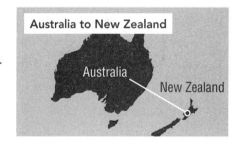
Australia to New Zealand
Australia
New Zealand

4. _____
   a. It's about 2,000 kilometers (1,200 miles).
   b. It's about 2,000 square kilometers.

the Amazon Rain Forest

5. _____
   a. It's 6 million square kilometers (2.5 million square miles).
   b. It's 6 million kilometers long.

the Grand Canyon

6. _____
   a. It's about 1.6 kilometers (1 mile) big.
   b. It's about 1.6 kilometers deep.

7 Answer these questions about your country.

1. How big is the largest city?

_____

2. What's the wettest month?

_____

3. What's the driest month?

_____

4. How hot does it get in the summer?

_____

5. How cold does it get in the winter?

_____

6. How high is the highest mountain?

_____

7. What's the most beautiful town to visit?

_____

8 Match the words with their opposites.

1. biggest _f_

2. bad ____

3. shorter ____

4. worse ____

5. worst ____

6. near ____

7. lowest ____

8. driest ____

9. hot ____

10. shortest ____

11. hotter ____

12. smaller ____

13. coldest ____

14. wetter ____

15. dry ____

16. high ____

a. better

b. wettest

c. colder

d. drier

e. hottest

f. smallest

g. far

h. bigger

i. good

j. best

k. low

l. highest

m. longest

n. wet

o. taller

p. cold

15 What are you doing later?

1 **Match the words in columns A and B. Write the names of the events.**

A	B	
✓ baseball	☐ appointment	**1.** baseball game
☐ birthday	☐ concert	**2.**
☐ car	✓ game	**3.**
☐ class	☐ match	**4.**
☐ medical	☐ party	**5.**
☐ rock	☐ race	**6.**
☐ tennis	☐ reunion	**7.**

2 **Read Joe's calendar and write about his plans each day. Use be going to.**

			Calendar			
+			Day Week Month Year			🔍

March
< This week >

Sunday	Monday	Tuesday	Wednesday	Thursday	Friday	Saturday
4	5	6	7	8	9	10
afternoon – play tennis with Brock	attend the managers' meeting at work	6:00 p.m. – see a movie with Angela	night – watch the soccer match with Annie and Bob	noon – have lunch with Paco	evening – go to the rock concert with friends	stay home and do laundry

1. On Sunday afternoon, Joe is going to play tennis with Brock.

2. _____

3. _____

4. _____

5. _____

6. _____

7. _____

3 **Complete this conversation. Use *be going to* and the verbs given.**

Stacey: What _____are_____ you _____going to do_____ this weekend, Hannah? (do)

Hannah: I _____ to a jazz concert on Saturday. (go)

Stacey: That sounds interesting.

Hannah: Yeah. There's a free concert in the park. What about you, Stacey?

Stacey: Well, Ryan and I _____ a baseball game in the afternoon. (see)

Hannah: And what _____ you _____ in the evening? (do)

Stacey: Ryan _____ his mother in the hospital. (visit) But I _____ not _____ anything really. (do)

Hannah: Well, I _____ some friends over for a barbecue. (have) Would you like to come?

Stacey: Thanks, I'd love to!

4 **Choose the correct responses.**

1. **A:** There's a basketball game on TV tonight. Do you want to watch it?

   B: _I'm sorry. I'm working late tonight._
   - How about this evening?
   - I'm sorry. I'm working late tonight.
   - Yes, it does.

2. **A:** Would you like to have dinner at Bella's Bistro tonight?

   B: _____
   - No, I'm not doing anything.
   - Sorry, I'm going away next week.
   - Yes, that sounds great! But it's my turn to pay.

3. **A:** Do you want to go hiking tomorrow?

   B: _____
   - Yes, I'm going to.
   - Can we go to a late show?
   - Sure, I'd love to.

4. **A:** How about going to a movie on Saturday?

   B: _____
   - Oh, I'm sorry. I can't.
   - Nothing special.
   - No, I wouldn't.

5 **Write invitations to this week's events in Eagleton.**

Exciting things to do this week in EAGLETON!

MONDAY	TUESDAY	WEDNESDAY	THURSDAY
Pop concert Ellie Goulding	**Summer Festival** Lots to do for everyone!	**Musical** Jersey Boys	**Museum** Modern art exhibition opening

1. *Are you doing anything on Monday evening? Do you want to see a pop concert?* OR
   I'm going to go to the Ellie Goulding concert on Monday. Would you like to come?

2. _____

3. _____

4. _____

6 **Write about how often you do these leisure activities. Use the expressions in the box.**

I . . . almost every weekend.
I never . . .
I often . . .
I sometimes . . . in the summer.
I . . . three or four times a year.

1. _____

2. _____

3. _____

4. _____

5. _____

6. _____

1 go to the park

2 go to concerts

3 have parties at home

4 see plays

5 watch horror movies

6 go on picnics

7 I need help!

A Read Hannah's social media post and the comments from her friends. Why does she need help?

Wall | Find friends | Chat | Profile | Sign out

Hannah   1h ago

Guess what? I'm moving! Is anyone around Saturday morning and (maybe?) afternoon to help me move things to my new apartment? I only have a few heavy things, but I could use all the help I can get. I'll provide pizza for dinner! Tell your friends and let me know!

Pablo   58 minutes ago

Cool, where are you moving? I wish I could help you Saturday, but I'm going to the beach. Don't hate me. I'm available on Sunday . . . but that probably doesn't help you. Sorry!

Richard   55 minutes ago

Congratulations on the new place! I can help, but not until the afternoon. My study group is getting together to prepare for the chemistry exam on Monday (yikes!). See you after lunch?

Lien   50 minutes ago

Whoo-hoo, new apartment! Saturday morning I have to go to my little brother's baseball tournament. But I'll come over right after it's finished. What's the address?

Kalil   42 minutes ago

I'm so sorry, Hannah. I'm going to be working all weekend. I know, bummer. Can't wait to visit, though. Save me a slice of pizza! I like leftovers. ;-)

Rachel   30 minutes ago

I can't wait to see your new apartment! I'm going to visit my grandmother all day, so unfortunately I can't come until the evening – probably when the pizza arrives! Hope that's OK . . .

Eliana   24 minutes ago

Oh, bad timing! I have the city bicycle race on Saturday morning. But I can come when it's over. In fact, I'm going to keep riding past the finish line and straight to your place! See you in the afternoon.

Daichi   15 minutes ago

Pizza?! I'm in. But wait. I need to drive my sister to her dance class and then to her basketball game. Argh. Can she move in with you? Just kidding. I'll be there by 3:00.

B Match Hannah's friends with their reasons for not being able to help her or for showing up to help late.

1. _____ has a bicycle race.   **a.** Daichi
2. _____ has to study.   **b.** Eliana
3. _____ has to drive his sister around.   **c.** Kalil
4. _____ is going to the beach.   **d.** Pablo
5. _____ is going to work all weekend.   **e.** Rachel
6. _____ is going to a baseball tournament.   **f.** Richard
7. _____ is going to visit her grandmother.   **g.** Lien

8 Read these messages. What did the caller say? Write the messages another way using *tell* or *ask*.

For: *Mr. Jones*

Message: *The meeting is at 10:30. Arrive 10 minutes early.*

1. Please tell Mr. Jones that the meeting is at 10:30.

   Could you ask him to arrive 10 minutes early?

For: *Ms. Rodriguez*

Message: *We need the report by noon. Call Ms. Brady as soon as possible.*

2. _____

   _____

For: Mr. Welch

Message: The new laptop is ready. Pick it up this afternoon.

3. _____

   _____

9 Look at the text messages. Write sentences asking someone to give these messages.

Grammar note: Negative infinitives

Request	Message
Don't call him today.	Please ask Jan **not to call** him today.
Don't go home yet.	Could you tell him **not to go** home yet?

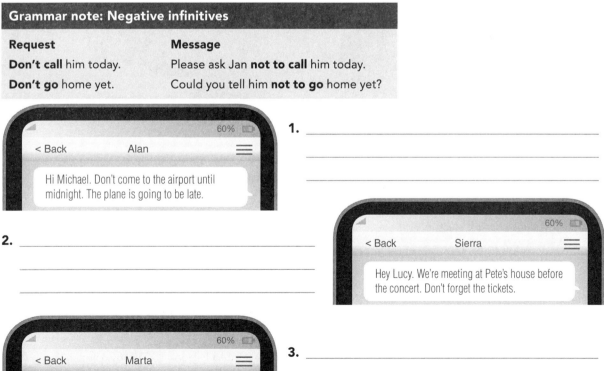

60%

< Back   Alan   ≡

Hi Michael. Don't come to the airport until midnight. The plane is going to be late.

1. _____

   _____

   _____

60%

< Back   Sierra   ≡

Hey Lucy. We're meeting at Pete's house before the concert. Don't forget the tickets.

2. _____

   _____

   _____

60%

< Back   Marta   ≡

Chris! The surprise party starts at noon. Don't be late!

3. _____

   _____

   _____

10 Choose the correct words.

Receptionist: Hello. McKenzie Corporation.

Mr. Brown: _____May I_____ speak to Mr. Scott Myers, please?
(May I / Would you)

Receptionist: I'm _____. He's not in. _____ a message?
(busy / sorry)   (Can I leave / Can I take)

Mr. Brown: Yes, please. This is Mr. Brown. _____ you _____
(Would / Please)   (tell him that / ask him to)

I have to reschedule our meeting? My phone number is 303-555-9001.

_____ you _____?
(Please / Could)   (ask him to call me / ask me to call him)

Receptionist: OK, Mr. Brown. I'll _____ the message.
(give him / tell him)

Mr. Brown: Thank you very much. Good-bye.

11 Match the questions with the correct responses.

☐ Let me see if she's in.	✓ That's OK. I'll call back.
☐ This is John. John Abrams.	☐ Sure, I'd love to come. Thanks.
☐ Oh, no. I don't eat meat.	☐ Yes. My number is 303-555-3241.

1. I'm sorry. She's busy at the moment.
   That's OK. I'll call back.

2. Could I ask her to call you back?
   _____

3. Who's calling, please?
   _____

4. Would you like to come to a party?
   _____

5. Could I speak to Tiffany, please?
   _____

6. Why don't we eat at Sam's Steakhouse tonight?
   _____

16 How have you changed?

1 Choose the correct responses.

1. A: Hey, you really look different.

    B: _Well, I've grown a mustache._

        • I moved into a new house.

        • I'm more outgoing than before.

        • Well, I've grown a mustache.

2. A: I haven't seen you for ages.

    B: _____

        • I know. How have you been?

        • Well, I got a bank loan.

        • My new job is more stressful.

3. A: You know, I have three kids now.

    B: _____

        • No, I haven't graduated from college yet.

        • Wow, I can't believe it!

        • Say, you've really changed your hair.

4. A: How are you?

    B: _____

        • I hope to get my driver's license soon.

        • Well, actually, I turned 18.

        • I'm doing really well.

2 Complete the sentences. Use information in the box and the present perfect.

☐ fall in love   ☐ get two pay raises   ☐ start an online course

1. JoAnn _____ this year. Now she has enough
money to buy a house.

2. Irvin _____. He's studying to become a
graphic designer.

3. Gisela and Russ _____. They're going to get
married in December.

3 Describe how these people have changed. Use the present or the past tense.

1. Mr. and Mrs. Kim <u>had a baby</u>. **2.** Sara _____.

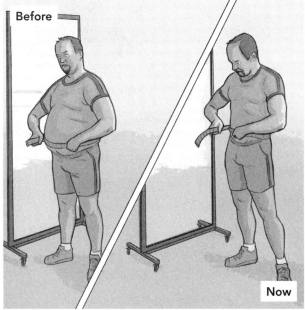

3. Ella _____. **4.** Ron _____.

4 Rewrite these sentences. Find another way to say each sentence using the words given.

1. I've grown out my hair.

   <u>My hair is longer now.</u>   (longer)

2. Raquel gained a lot of weight.

   _____ (heavier)

3. Ben goes to a new school now.

   _____ (change)

4. Helen and George got divorced last year.

   _____ (married)

5. Traci quit eating fast food.

   _____ (healthier)

6. We quit working out at the gym.

   _____ (not go)

5 Life changes

A Read the passages on the left in part B. Complete these sentences.

1. _____ had an interesting job two years ago.
2. _____ had money problems two years ago.
3. _____ was a student two years ago.

B Now read the passages on the right. Match the people's lives two years ago with their lives now.

Rafael

Diane and her husband

Krystina

Two years ago	Now
1. Rafael Two years ago, I was a student, and I thought life was really good. I got up late. I spent the day talking to friends, and then I studied all night. I wore jeans and sweatshirts and had long hair and a beard. I felt free. _____	**a.** Now my life has completely changed. I got married six months ago! My husband and I often have friends over for dinner. We're taking classes several nights a week. It's great! We're even talking about starting a family soon.
2. Diane I moved to a new town two years ago. My job was interesting, but I was single and I didn't have any friends. People at work were friendly but not very outgoing. We never did anything after work. _____	**b.** Now I work as a computer programmer for an international company. I've moved to Seoul and have started to learn Korean. Korean food is great, and I've gained a few pounds. I feel much happier and healthier.
3. Krystina My life seemed to come to an end two years ago. I lost my job. Then I lost weight and looked terrible. Money became a problem. I was very sad. I needed some good luck. _____	**c.** Now I actually look forward to getting up early in the morning and going to work. Of course, I dress up now, and my hair is shorter. But I don't really mind. At least my evenings are free!

C Underline at least two changes in each person's life.

6 Complete the sentences. Use the words in the box.

| ☐ broke | ☐ graduation | ☐ responsibilities |
| ☐ career | ☑ loan | ☐ successful |

1. Rhonda wants to pay off her student ____loan____ before she buys a car.

2. I'd like to be _____ in my first job. Then I can get a better job and a raise.

3. I go to school, and I have a family and a part-time job. I have a lot of _____.

4. After _____, Amelia and Lee plan to look for jobs.

5. Max lost his job. Now he's _____, and he can't pay his rent.

6. What _____ are you most interested in pursuing?

7 Complete this conversation. Use the words given.

Mariko: What ____do you plan to do____ (plan, do) this summer, Brian?

Brian: I _____ (want, get) a summer job.
I _____ (like, save) money for a vacation.

Mariko: Really? Where _____ (like, go)?

Brian: I _____ (love, travel) to Latin America.
What about you, Mariko?

Mariko: Well, I _____ (not go, get) a job right away. First, I _____ (want, go) to Spain and Portugal.

Brian: Sounds great, but how _____ (go, pay) for it?

Mariko: I _____ (hope, borrow) some money from my brother. I have a good excuse. I _____ (plan, take) courses in Spanish and Portuguese.

Brian: Oh, I'm tired of studying!

Mariko: I love to study. I also _____ (hope, take) people on tours to Latin America. Why don't you come on my first tour?

Brian: Count me in!

8 **Imagine you have these problems. Write three sentences about changing your situation. Use the words in the box.**

1. I just moved to a new town, and I don't know anyone. I never do anything after work. People at work don't really talk to me. I haven't had a date in about four months. And I never find anything fun to do on the weekends.

> I'm going to . . .   I want to . . .   I plan to . . .

_____

_____

_____

_____

2. I've become less careful about my health lately. I've stopped jogging because I'm bored with it. I've started eating more fast food because I'm too tired to cook after work. And I can't sleep at night.

> I'm going to . . .   I'd like to . . .   I'd love to . . .

_____

_____

_____

_____

3. My job is so boring. I spend two hours driving to and from work every day, and I don't make enough money! I can't find a new job, though, because of my poor computer skills.

> I hope to . . .   I want to . . .   I plan to . . .

_____

_____

_____

_____

9 **Choose the correct words to complete each sentence. Use the correct form of the word and add any words if necessary.**

1. Floyd hopes to _____move_____ to a small town.
   (move / live / change)

2. This job is _____ my last job.
   (outgoing / stressful / crowded)

3. After graduation, Kira plans _____ for an international company.
   (play / work / move)

4. Stephanie's salary is much _____ before. She had to take a pay cut.
   (low / short / high)

5. I hope to buy a house soon. I need _____ a bank loan.
   (open / start / get)

6. Neil and Kelly got _____ last summer. The wedding will be in April.
   (engage / marry)

10 **Advise people how to make changes in their lives. Use expressions like the ones in the box.**

| Why don't you . . .   You should . . .   You shouldn't . . . |

1. I've gained a lot of weight this year.
   _____

2. My hair is longer, but it doesn't look good.
   _____

3. I've gotten tired of wearing the same old clothes.
   _____

4. I want to start a successful business.
   _____

5. I'm often bored on weekends.
   _____

6. I don't really have any goals.
   _____

7. I've finished this textbook, but I still want to improve my English!
   _____